The Federalist Papers, Number 86

Norwood

Nilsson

Call

Friends of Freedom

The Federalist Papers, Number 86

The Treaty Clause

James Ervin Norwood

The General Welfare Clause

George W. Nilsson

Government by Decree through Executive Agreement

Joseph L. Call

Prepaid price: $12 plus $3 shipping and handling and $1.20 tax.
(Tax is on sales in Texas only.)

Friends of Freedom Publishers

P.O. Box 6124
Waco, Texas 76706-0124
1-817-662-4643

1-800-356-4897 for orders

All major credit cards are accepted.

Friends of Freedom Publishers is dedicated to the victory of capitalism and individualism and to the defeat of communism and collectivism. Friends of Freedom is pledged to induce an understanding of the above concepts, so that people know what they are for and what they are against.

Library of Congress Cataloging-in-Publication Data

Norwood, James Ervin, 1915-
  The Federalist Papers, Number 86

   Includes bibliographies, appendices, and indices.
   Contents: "The Treaty Clause," James Ervin Norwood; "The General Welfare Clause," George W. Nilsson; "Government by Decree through Executive Agreement," Joseph L. Call.
   1. Treaty-making power – United States – History. 2. United States – Foreign relations – Executive agreements – History. 3. United States – Constitutional law – Welfare clause – History. 4. Right of property – United States – History. 5. United States – Politics and government – 20th century. I. Nilsson, George W., 1890-1974. II. Call, Joseph L., 1903- . III. Title.
KF5055.N67   1988   342.73'0412   87-24651
ISBN 0-915854-87-2   347.302412

Contents

Appendices

Indices

From His Farewell Address

. . . If in the opinion of the people the distribution or modification of the constitutional powers be in any particular wrong, let it be corrected by an amendment in the way which the Constitution designates. But let there be no change by usurpation; for though this in one instance may be the instrument for good, it is the customary weapon by which free governments are destroyed. The precedent must always greatly overbalance in permanent evil any partial or transient benefit which the use can at any time yield.

George Washington

Preface

The conventional wisdom holds that treaty law is the law of the land, in spite of anything in the Constitution to the contrary. The idea that treaty law is privileged to contradict the Constitution and to prevail over it is utterly false. "The Treaty Clause" will show why treaty law must conform to the Constitution, at least as it applies to American citizens and their property and to the activities of their Government.

It is also widely believed that Congressional legislation that executes treaties can violate the Constitution. Although this has happened, such legislation is unconstitutional. "The Treaty Clause" will show that legislation to execute treaties must conform to the Constitution.

"The Treaty Clause" reigns in the implied powers of the Federal Government to Chief Justice Marshall's limits in *McCullough* v. *Maryland*. It also hauls in *Marbury* v. *Madison* to Marshall's boundaries.

It is incorrectly believed that the General Welfare Clause gives the Federal Government a wide range of unenumerated powers. "The General Welfare Clause" will show that there is no power in the Clause.

"Government by Decree through Executive Agreement" further develops some of the points in "The Treaty Clause" and presents some additional facts on treaty law.

Since each part of this work is progressively organized and since the work as a whole is so organized, it is recommended that one read it serially and that one read the notes as they are called out. Only after reading it serially, should one skip around in it. If one does not read serially, one could lose the thread of thought, especially in "The Treaty Clause." ("The Treaty Clause" is easy to read, if you read it serially and cover the notes as they are cited.)

About the Authors

James Ervin Norwood researches and writes in the areas of American constitutional law, Austrian neo-classical free market economics, and classical liberal political science.

One objective of his research and writing is to integrate law with free market economics through negation amendments to the Constitution, so that law cannot block applications of free market economics. He believes that, with law and free market economics in separate containers intellectually and with law contradicting free market economics, neither they nor civilization will survive.

He sees positive government power as an opening through which people can go to impose their values on each other to establish conflict and tyranny and to destroy property rights, economy, and civilization.

George W. Nilsson graduated from Northwestern University Law School. He practiced in Arizona from 1915 to 1924 and practiced in California during the rest of his career. In 1961, he was a member of the Committee on American Citizenship of the American Bar Association. He was also active in the ABA in the work of the Section of Mineral and Natural Resources Law.

Joseph L. Call graduated from the University of Southern California Law School in 1925. He was the Presiding Judge of the Municipal Court, Los Angeles Judicial District, for some twenty years.

Words of Appreciation

I am indebted to Judge Joseph L. Call, George W. Nilsson, Dr. V. Orval Watts, Judge William J. Palmer, Chief Justice John Marshall, Dr. Murray N. Rothbard, Dr. Ludwig von Mises, and the authors of *The Federalist Papers*, Alexander Hamilton, James Madison, and John Jay. Although my insights and conclusions are my responsibility, I could have scarcely approached the subject as either editor or contributor without their thoughts at hand.

Lucia Backus of the Waco-McLennan County Library did an indispensable and sometimes difficult job of rounding up books through the Interlibrary Loan Service. Her help made possible complete and accurate citations in many instances. The books that she found enabled me to include quotations that, in my judgement, have enriched this work and your reading pleasure considerably.

JEN

Editor

Foreword

Thomas Paine

If one wonders what the Founding Fathers would write in the face of today's blatant departures from the Constitution, *The Federalist Papers, Number 86* is your answer. As a student of the original *Federalist Papers*, I believe that the three essays that follow definitely continue the series in a manner consistent with the first eighty-five *Federalist Papers*.

It is my judgement that, should you take these extraordinary writings seriously and follow up by reading the excellent appendices and pursuing the avenues of research that are offered, we will be off to a glorious new start with the Constitution that was and must again be, if we are to regain our freedom.

It is also my estimate that from such studies we will restore property rights to a large degree and thereby make an endurable peace and prosperity not only possible but probable. Although prosperity is not a necessary prerequisite for peace, it is certain that the peace that is supported by respect for property rights is a prerequisite for prosperity. A diligent pursuit of this seminal volume and scholarship with its references offers you both peace and prosperity, as a result of respect for property rights.

Now is the time for us to make history, as our Forefathers did with their similar endeavor in the First American

Revolution. For the Second American Revolution, we must reconstruct two ships: the U.S.S. Constitution and the U.S.S. Free Enterprise. Fortunately, we have the materials at hand to do the job and the people to use the materials.

We have a long voyage to make and a difficult passage; but, with sustained study, we will save the day for ourselves and our posterity and see the rebirth of Liberty in our time.

To the Constitution

The Federalist Papers,

Number 86

The Treaty Clause

James Ervin Norwood

To restore huge portions of our once great Constitution and to reinstate federalism to some degree, an examination of Clause 1, Paragraph 2, Article VI, United States Constitution, and various interpretations of it are in order.

Clause 1, Paragraph 2, Article VI, reads as follows:

"This Constitution, and the Laws of the United States which shall be made in Pursuance thereof; and all Treaties made, or which shall be made, under the Authority of the United States, shall be the supreme Law of the Land. . . ."

A correct reading of the Treaty Clause would refute the notion that a treaty can nullify any portion of the Constitution. However, majorities of the United States Supreme Court have proved in many rulings that they cannot read and understand the English language, which ability is prerequisite to correct interpretation of the late Constitution. Numerous authorities on constitutional law can support this assertion regarding inability to read, including astonished minorities of the U.S. Supreme Court in many rulings of the Court.

A key phrase in reading the Treaty Clause is "under the Authority of the United States. . . ." Since the United States Government, meaning the Executive branch in this discussion, gains its lawful authority solely from the Con-

1

stitution, it follows that any treaty that it makes in violation of the Constitution is unauthorized. The United States Government has no lawful authority to act in violation of or in excess of the Constitution. Any action by it in violation of or in excess of the Constitution is unconstitutional and patently unlawful.

How some majorities of the Supreme Court have gradually perverted the Treaty Clause to mean something entirely different from its true meaning is an interesting study in lawlessness. A few examples are appropriate.

In *Missouri v. Holland*, 252 U.S. 416, 64 L. Ed. 641, 40 S. Ct. 382 (1920), the majority of the Supreme Court ruled that a treaty with Great Britain to protect migratory birds in the U.S. and Canada gave Congress legislative power that had been previously ruled unconstitutional.[1] The ruling was based partially on a misreading of the Treaty Clause by the majority, which failure to read and comprehend the English language enabled it to ignore the fact that action by the Executive branch that is unauthorized by the Constitution is unlawful. The majority ruled: "Acts of Congress are the supreme law of the land only when made in pursuance of the Constitution, while treaties are declared to be so when made under the authority of the United States." (252 U.S. 433, 64 L. Ed. 647-648, 40 S. Ct. 383.) The failure of the majority to understand that the United States Government has no authority, except that authority granted to it by the People in the enumeration of powers in the Constitution, and that it cannot act lawfully in violation of the Constitution resulted in the Court's error.

> . . . We do not mean to imply that there are no qualifications to the treaty-making power; but they must be ascertained in a different way [than

2

by reference to the constitutional limitations of Government power]. It is obvious that there may be matters of the sharpest *exigency* [italics added] for the national well being that an act of Congress could not deal with [because of the unconstitutional nature of the legislation that the matter would require,] but that a treaty followed by such an act could, and it is not lightly to be assumed that, in matters requiring national action, "a power which must belong to and somewhere reside in every civilized government" is not to be found. . . . [When you untangle that one, the Court said that the Congress and the Government derive powers that are not enumerated to them in the Constitution from the fact that other civilized governments have such powers. This is an unconstitutional assumption by the Court and it is an unconstitutional assignment of power by the Court to the Congress and the Government and to itself.] With regard to that we may add that when we are dealing with words that also are a constituent act, like the Constitution of the United States, we must realize that they have called into life a being the development of which could not have been foreseen completely by the most gifted of its begetters. It was enough for them to realize or to hope that they had created an organism; it has taken a century and has cost their successors much sweat and blood to prove that they created a nation. *The case before us must be considered in the light of our whole experience and not merely what was*

3

said a hundred years ago. [Italics added. 252 U.S. 433, 64 L. Ed. 648, 40 S. Ct. 383.]

Justices Van Devanter and Pitney dissented against this naked and bold unconstitutional expansion of the enumeration of powers in the Constitution, as the Signers of the Constitution would have.

To examine some of the majority's flagrant flights from the Constitution, we should begin with President Theodore Roosevelt's evasion of the Constitution. Once upon a time his State Department negotiated a treaty with the Dominican Republic. When the Senate refused to ratify the treaty, he put it into effect through an exchange of diplomatic notes with the Dominican Republic.[2] The result was an executive agreement that was entered into force as law on April 1, 1905.[3]

For an executive agreement that is entered into without Congressional authorization to lawfully have the force of a treaty, it must have the consent of two-thirds of the Senate present; otherwise the Executive branch is legislating by decree. (Although this essay in some places assumes [to facilitate discussion relevant to precedents but with debate to the contrary], that preauthorization of an executive agreement by Congress would give it the force of a treaty, strictly speaking such preauthorization would have to include a Senatorial majority of two-thirds of the members present to constitutionally give an executive agreement the power of a treaty. Otherwise, the President could obtain a preauthorization by simple majorities of the House and Senate to effect an executive agreement having treaty power that he could not get consent to by two-thirds of the Senate present.)

Aside from the considerable fact that Theodore

Roosevelt's deadly unconstitutional precedent has been used by the Executive branch many times to haul off your wealth, security, and constitutional rights, the Supreme Court bought his unconstitutional usurpation of power in *U.S. v. Belmont* and in *U.S. v. Pink* (both of which are cited and discussed below), by ruling that an executive agreement that has neither the consent of two-thirds of the Senate present nor preauthorization by Congress has the status of a treaty.[4]

In *U.S. v. Belmont*, 301 U.S. 324, 81 L. Ed. 1134, 57 S. Ct. 758 (1937), the majority of the Supreme Court gave an executive agreement between President Franklin D. Roosevelt and Maxim Litvinov, People's Commissar for Foreign Affairs of the U.S.S.R., the force of a treaty, even though Congress had not given the President its preapproval, as in Section 3 of the Tariff act of 1897 (which Section is discussed in Note 4), and even though the agreement was not ratified by two-thirds of the Senate present.[5] Justice Sutherland wrote in the majority opinion: "The assignment and agreements in connection therewith did not, as in the case of treaties, as that term is used in the treaty making clause of the Constitution (Article II, Section 2), require the advice and consent of the Senate." He went to *B. Altman & Co. v. United States* (which is cited and discussed in Note 4), to find his definition of a treaty as "a compact made between two or more independent nations, with a view to the public welfare." He then continued, as follows: "But an international compact, as this was, is not always a treaty which requires the participation of the Senate." (301 U.S. 330, 81 L. Ed. 1139, 57 S. Ct. 761.) If such a compact is to have constitutionally the force of law of a treaty, it must have either been preauthorized by Congress (according to questionable precedents), or have been consented to by two-thirds of the Senate present.

After giving the agreement the force of a treaty and stating that it is not a treaty that requires the consent of the Senate, Justice Sutherland then contradicted his reasoning that the agreement does not require the consent of the Senate, by citing *B. Altman & Co. v. United States* (infra, Note 4), as authority:

> . . . There are many such compacts, of which a protocol, a modus vivendi, a postal convention, and agreements like that now under consideration are illustrations. . . . The distinction was pointed out by this court in the Altman Case, supra, which arose under Section 3 of the Tariff Act of 1897 [130 Stat. 151, 203], authorizing the President to conclude commercial agreements with foreign countries in certain specified matters. We held that although this might not be a treaty requiring ratification by the Senate, it was a compact negotiation and proclaimed under the authority of the President, [which authority was explicitly granted to him by Congress in Section 3 of the Act,] *and as such was a "treaty"*. . . . [301 U.S. 330-331, 81 L. Ed. 1139, 57 S. Ct. 761.]

Although the Senate in the matter, above, did not act alone after the executive agreement was made, it acted with the House to preapprove the President's action.

Justice Sutherland again contradicted himself, as follows:

"Plainly, the external powers of the United States are

to be exercised without regard to state laws or policies. The supremacy of a treaty in this respect has been recognized from the beginning." (301 U.S. 331, 81 L. Ed. 1139, 57 S. Ct. 761.) The compact that was not a treaty requiring the ratification of the Senate, with the stroke of Justice Sutherland's pen, became a treaty that is supreme, which supremacy can come only from consent of two-thirds of the Senate present.

First, he said that an executive agreement is not a treaty and does not require the consent of the Senate. Then he cited the Altman Case, as giving an executive agreement the force of a treaty; but he neglected to contrast the fact that the agreement by President Theodore Roosevelt was authorized by Congress with the fact that the agreement by President Franklin D. Roosevelt was not authorized by Congress. (Although the President has the right to recognize any government, he has no right to attach to such recognition an executive agreement that becomes the law of the land as a treaty, without the consent of two-thirds of the Senate present to that agreement or pre-authorization by the Congress for that agreement [with the majority in the Senate being two-thirds of the Senate present].)

Justice Sutherland even quoted a contemporary English court decision as somehow giving authority to our Government that is not granted to it by the People in the Constitution. (A. M. Luther v. James Sagor and Co., L.R. [1921] 3 K.B. 532.) Immediately following the quotes, he wrote, "Futher citation of authority seems unnecessary."[6] (301 U.S. 330, 81 L. Ed. 1139, 57 S. Ct. 760.)

In United States v. Pink, 315 U.S. 203, 86 L. Ed. 796, 62 S. Ct. 552 (1942), the majority fell back on the erroneous ruling in *United States* v. *Belmont*, supra.[7] Chief Justice Stone wrote in the dissent of the minority the following:

> I shall state my grounds for thinking that the pronouncements in the Belmont case, on which the Court relies for the answer to these questions, are without the support of reason or accepted principles of law. [315 U.S. 244, 86 L. Ed. 825, 62 S. Ct. 572.]
>
> This Court has repeatedly decided that the extent to which a state court will follow the rules of law of a recognized foreign country in preference to its own is wholly a matter of comity, and that in the absence of relevant treaty obligations the application in the courts of a state of its own rules of law rather than those of a foreign country raises no federal question. [315 U.S. 245, 86 L. Ed. 826, 62 S. Ct. 572.]
>
> . . . They have compelled the state to surrender its own rules of law applicable to property within its limits, and to substitute rules of Russian law for them. . . . [315 U.S. 248, 86 L. Ed. 827, 62 S. Ct. 574.]
>
> I assume for present purposes that these sweeping alterations of the rights of states and of persons could be achieved by treaty or even executive agreement [if such treaty or agreement is not in violation of the Constitution], although we are referred to no authority which would sustain such an exercise of power as is said to have been exerted here by mere assignment unratified by the Senate. [315 U.S. 249, 86 L. Ed. 828,

62 S. Ct. 574.]

We are not pointed to anything on the face of the documents or in the diplomatic correspondence which even suggests that the United States was to be placed in a better position with respect to the claim which it now asserts, than was the Soviet Government and nationals. Nor is there any intimation in them that recognition was to give to prior public acts of the Soviet Government any greater extraterritorial effect than attaches to such acts occurring after recognition – acts which by the common understanding of English and American courts are ordinarily deemed to be without extraterritorial force, and which in any event have never before been considered to restrict the power of the states to apply their own rules of law to foreign-owned property within their territory. [315 U.S. 251, 86 L. Ed. 829, 62 S. Ct. 575.]

. . . But, until now, recognition of a foreign government by this Government has never been thought to serve as a full faith and credit clause compelling obedience here to the laws and public acts of the recognized government with respect to property and transactions in this country. One could as well argue that by the Soviet Government's recognition of our own government, which accompanied the transactions now under consideration, it had undertaken to apply in Russia the New York law applicable to Russian property in New York. [315 U.S. 251-252, 86 L. Ed. 829, 62 S. Ct. 575.]

. . . The practical consequences of the present decision seem to be, in every case of recognition of a foreign government, to foist upon the executive the responsibility for subordinating domestic to foreign law in conflicts cases, whether intended or not, unless such a purpose is affirmatively disclaimed. [315 U.S. 256, 86 L. Ed. 831-832, 62 S. Ct. 577.]

In *U.S. v. Belmont*, supra, and in *U.S. v. Pink*, supra, the majority cited *U.S. v. Curtiss-Wright Export Corporation*, 299 U.S. 304, 81 L. Ed. 255, 57 S. Ct. 216 (1936), for authority. However in *U.S. v. Curtiss-Wright*, supra, the President was acting on authority granted to him by a Joint Resolution of Congress.[8] The majority in each case (*U.S. v. Belmont*, supra, and *U.S. v. Pink*, supra), declared that Presidential action that was not authorized by Congress, that was not within the enumerated powers of the Executive branch, and that was not consented to by the Senate as required by Clause 1, Paragraph 2, Section 2, Article II, U.S. Constitution, to be the "law of the land."[9]

I offer the observation that a treaty or executive agreement that is made by the United States Government outside of its constitutional authority to act is the law of nothing – *i.e.*, it is lawless. I believe that Hamilton, Madison, and Jay would concur, as would the Founders who signed their names to the Constitution with Hamilton and Madison.

The Constitution is what it says it is, which is to say that it is what its Signers said it is, with due respect for amendments adopted in accord with Article V.[10] Many of its Signers were lawyers and were not given to affixing their names to documents that were ambiguous to them. (A study of their ideological premises of the natural rights of man, which are reflected in the Declaration of Independence, would explain a lot to those who claim that they cannot determine the intent of the Framers. That they do not understand and appreciate the morality and the utility of natural rights is their fault, not the fault of the Founders who enshrined the legality of natural rights in our basic Law.) In laying the tracks of nationhood, they quite naturally took extra care as to the meanings and legal effects of the Document to which they signed their names.[11] The Constitution is what the States have subscribed to, with special care as to its meanings and legal effects. The mystery is not the meaning of the Constitution. The question is why more scholars and Supreme Court Justices, not to mention others in the judiciary, have not studied it and respected it as thoroughly as John Marshall did.

It follows that all treaties that are outside of *Marbury v. Madison* or *McCullough v. Maryland* (as discussed in Note 10), outside of Marshall's dissent in *Ogden v. Saunders* (infra, Note 10), outside of the authority granted by the People to the United States Government through the Constitution, or outside of the consent of two-thirds of the Senate present are null and void and should be so declared by the majority of the Supreme Court at every opportunity to rule on them. It also follows that executive agreements that are not approved as above or that are not preauthorized by Congress, with the majority in the Senate being two-thirds of the Senate present, are in the same unconstitutional category and should be so condemned and declared without the effect of treaties by the majority of the Supreme Court in every instance.[12]

11

The Constitution is not what a number of anarchic Supreme Court Justices have projected into it, as expressions of their personal predilections, their socialist miseducations, their disrespect for property rights and thus human rights, their almost total lack of understanding of free market economics as an interpretive tool in defining property rights and recognizing their protection and sanctity under Amendment V of the Constitution, and their lack of appreciation for the great ideas of classical liberalism that the Drafters inscribed in the Document from the works of John Locke and others.

Although *stare decisis* has the force of law until it is reversed or superseded, *stare decisis* can be unconstitutional and often is unconstitutional. *i.e.*, The majority of the Supreme Court can rule unconstitutionally and has done so many times, sometimes by mistake and sometimes by design. One must keep in mind that, regardless of the lawless wanderings of the Supreme Court from the Constitution into the unbounded swamps of strange isms, the Constitution remains the Law.[13]

As the Constitution arose from the minds of great thinkers, it can only be maintained by the minds of great thinkers, not only on the Supreme Court but all throughout the Land. The Rule of Law cannot be nourished by nine alone. Its further construction and enhancement is a Great Enterprise for all who can take in some degree the responsibility to read, write, study, and think toward that end. Why should we care? The pages of history, including the pages of our own history, are splattered with blood from the terrible alternatives to the Law of the Constitution.[14]

Notes

[1]The law dealing with migratory birds that was ruled unconstitutional was passed by Congress in 1913. (37 Stat. 828, 847-848.)

The cases in which the law was ruled unconstitutional are *U.S. v. Shauver*, 214 F. 154 (1914); *U.S. v. McCullagh*, *Same v. Savage*, and *Same v. Sapp*, 221 F. 288 (1915); and *State v. Sawyer*, 113 Me. 458, 94 A. 886 (1915).

The treaty between Great Britain and the United States, entitled "Convention between Great Britain and the United States for the Protection of Migratory Birds," was signed on August 16, 1916, and went into effect upon the exchange of ratifications on December 7, 1916. (Clive Parry [ed. and annot.], *The Consolidated Treaty Series* [Dobbs Ferry, New York: Oceana Publications, 1981], CCXXI, p. 408.)

The "Migratory Bird Treaty Act" to execute the above treaty was passed by Congress in 1918. (40 Stat. 755-757.)

[2]Dana Gardner Monroe, "Dominican Republic," *Encyclopedia Britannica*, Vol. VII, 1964 ed.; and Wilfred E. Binkley and Malcolm C. Moos, *A Grammar of American Politics: The National Government* (3rd ed. rev.; New York: Alfred A Knoph, Inc., 1958), pp. 316-317.

[3]The title of this agreement is "Collection and Disbursement of Customs Revenues." (Parry, *op. cit.* [1980], CXCVIII, p. 208.)

[4]In no way did Congress authorize the President to enter into such an executive agreement, in which case the agreement would indeed be the equivalent of a treaty and would be treaty law under the reversible precedent set in the Altman Case (infra). With respect to an executive

agreement with France that the President made in regard to tariffs under authority granted to him by Congress in Section 3 of the Tariff Act of 1897, the Supreme Court said in *B. Altman & Co. v. United States*, 224 U.S. 583, 56 L. Ed. 894, 32 S. Ct. 593 (1912):

> . . . While it may be true that this commercial agreement made under authority of the tariff act of 1897, Section 3, was not a treaty possessing the dignity of one requiring ratification by the Senate of the United States, it was an international compact, negotiated between the representatives of two sovereign nations, and made in the name and on behalf of the contracting countries, and dealing with important commercial relations between the two countries, and was proclaimed by the President. If not technically a treaty requiring ratification, nevertheless it was a compact authorized by the Congress of the United States, negotiated and proclaimed under the authority of its President. We think such a compact is a treaty. . . . [224 U.S. 601, 56 L. Ed. 910, 32 S. Ct. 597.]

Under the above authority, the President has the advice and consent of the entire Congress, not just the advice and consent of the Senate. It is worth noting that, had Congress granted the President such authority in the matter with the Dominican Republic, he would not have submitted the matter to the Senate for its consent, as such submission would have been superfluous to authority already granted and would have exposed it to second thoughts or reconsideration and disapproval.

In Section 3 of the Act, Congress authorized the President to "enter into negotiations with the governments of those countries exporting to the United States the above-mentioned articles, or any of them, with a view to the arrangement of commercial agreements in which reciprocal and equivalent concessions may be secured in favor of the products and manufacturers of the United States. . . ." (30 Stat. 203.)

[5] The background for *U.S.* v. *Belmont*, infra, and *U.S.* v. *Pink*, infra, is as follows:

The Soviets had a string of debts that they owed to the United States. They disputed the validity of some of these debts, particularly the debts that they knew that they could not pay. They were able and willing to pay the small debts; but they neglected to do so, believing that such action would have validated all of the debts. (Department of State Publication 4539, "Recognition by the United States of the Soviet Union, November 16, 1933," *Foreign Relations of the United States: The Soviet Union, 1933-1939* [Washington: United States Government Printing Office, 1952], p. 3.)

It was also the case that Russian nationals had interests in Russian corporations in the United States (which corporations were operating in the United States at the time of the Red takeover of Russia in 1917), and that these nationals had title to the deposits of the corporations in the U.S. banks.

Since the Soviets had issued decrees seizing the private property of Russian nationals at home and abroad, it held all such property to be the property of the Soviet Government. It held that, in the United States, Russian law (*i.e.*, communist "law"), not the laws of our various states and our constitutional law, must be applied to such property.

To facilitate recognition of the Soviet Union by the United States, a means and a policy to settle these and other claims and counter claims had to be indicated by the Soviets. This was done, in part, with the Litvinov Assignment on November 16, 1933, the date of recognition. In it Maxim Litvinov, People's Commissar for Foreign Affairs, U.S.S.R., assigned to the United States Government any Soviet interests in property held by Russian nationals in the United States and any Soviet interests in any claims by Russian nationals against the U.S. Government (*Russian Volunteer Fleet v. United States*, 68 C. Cls. 32 [1929], 282 U.S. 481, 75 L. Ed. 473, 51 S. Ct. 229 [1931].)

Thus, the United States Government became a partner-in-crime with the gang of psychopathic criminals that composed the Soviet Government, in the confiscation of the property of friendly foreigners on American soil. This unconstitutional position was taken by executive agreement, in spite of Amendment V, U.S. Constitution, and in nullification of the U.S. Supreme Court's ruling that friendly aliens have the protection of Amendment V for their property in the United States in *Russian Volunteer Fleet v. United States*, supra.

When events had evolved to *U.S. v. Belmont*, supra, and *U.S. v. Pink*, infra, the Litvinov Assignment was relied upon as extraconstitutional law by the United States to seize the property of friendly Russian aliens in the United States.

A complete reading of all of the above references will fill in the gaps in this necessarily brief account of a rather complex situation. In essence, we did for the communists what they were powerless to do for themselves; and we gave them the additional advantage of the further destruc-

what they were powerless to do for themselves; and we gave them the additional advantage of the further destruction of our Constitution. The perfidy would have been just as unconstitutional had two-thirds of the Senate present or all of the Senate and all of the House approved of the Litvinov Assignment.

[6]Preceding this statement, Justice Sutherland wrote:

. . . The court regarded the decree as one of confiscation, but was unable to see (Bankes, L.J., p. 546) how the courts could treat the decree "otherwise than as the expression by the de facto government of a civilized country of a policy which it considered to be in the best interest of that country. It must be quite immaterial for present purposes that the same views are not entertained by the Government of this country, are repudiated by the vast majority of its citizens, and are not recognized by our laws." Lord Justice Scrutton, in his opinion, discusses (pp. 557-559) the contention that the courts should refuse to recognize the decree and the titles derived under it as confiscatory and unjust, and concludes that the question is one not for judges but for the action of the sovereign through his ministers. "I do not feel able," he said [p. 559] "to come to the conclusion that the legislation of a state [the Russian Federated Socialist Republic] recognized by *my Sovereign* as an independent sovereign state is so contrary to moral principle that the judges ought not to recognize it. [This was said in regard to the bloody seizures by the Bolsheviks in Russia after they came to power in their October Revolu-

17

each rests on the political advisers of the Sovereign and not on the judges." [Italics added. 301 U.S. 329-330, 81 L. Ed. 1138-1139, 57 S. Ct. 760.]

Justice Sutherland could have considered that in this country the People are Sovereign, not the President and his administrators, and that that Sovereignty is expressed in writing in the Preamble to the Constitution of the United States and in the second paragraph of the Declaration of Independence. By simply quoting those expressions of the Sovereignty of the People, he could have disposed of the issue at hand rather rapidly. (Although they have no force of law, they certainly represent the intent of the Signers of the Constitution.) He chose, instead, to impose a doctrine of monarchial sovereignty upon us that we had rejected from the beginning of our Nationhood, whether it be applied to us by tyrants from abroad or by domestic despots.

It comes to mind that we fought and won a war to enforce the fact that the People are Sovereign and that we wrote a Constitution that is styled as the Law of the Land to make that fact stick. The Supreme Court is bound by that Law, as well as the Executive branch and the Legislative branch. The Supreme Court is not at liberty to amend that Document. Only the People in their sovereign capacity can lawfully amend the Constitution.

[7]In the "Opinion of the Court" in *U.S. v. Pink*, supra, Justice Douglas wrote:

. . . A treaty is the "Law of the Land" under the supremacy clause, Art. VI, Cl. 2, of the Constitution. Such international compacts and agreements as the Litvinov Assignment have a similar dignity. [315 U.S. 230, 86 L. Ed. 818, 62 S. Ct. 565.]

Since he could find absolutely no authority in the Constitution for his equation of a treaty that is consented to by two-thirds of the Senate present with an international compact or agreement that is not consented to by two-thirds of the Senate present, he built error upon error by citing *U.S. v. Belmont*, supra, for authority. (*Ibid.*) He even cited (*ibid.*) a contemporary writer (Edward S. Corwin, *The President: Office and Powers* [New York: New York University Press, 1940], pp. 228-240), for his "authorization" to circumvent the Constitution. (It is worth commenting upon that Corwin released the second revised edition of his book in 1941, the third revised edition in 1948, and the fourth revised edition in 1957. An examination of this work in its several editions indicates that the author kept up to date with the Supreme Court, as it revised the Constitution to expand Presidential powers.) He even had the audacity to inappropriately cite *The Federalist Papers*, Number 64. (*Ibid.*)

Having put forth his unconstitutional equation as "the law of the land," Brother Douglas continued his pitch to sell his fraudulent equation, as follows:

> . . . But state law must yield when it is inconsistent with or impairs the policy or provisions of a treaty or of an international compact or agreement. . . . [315 U.S. 230-231, 86 L. Ed. 818, 62 S. Ct 566.] Then the power of a state to refuse enforcement of rights based on foreign law which runs counter to the public policy of the forum. . . must give way before the superior Federal policy evidenced by a treaty or interna-

19

tional compact or agreement. [315 U.S. 231, 86 L. Ed. 818, 62 S. Ct. 566.]

[8]This statement does not accept as constitutional the precedent that a simple majority of the Senate in conjunction with a simple majority of the House gives an executive agreement the power of a treaty.

Neither does this statement accept Justice Sutherland's audacious amendment of the Constitution to conform to his personal viewpoints.

In the decision of the majority, Justice Sutherland wrote:

> . . . The broad statement that the federal government can exercise no powers except those specifically enumerated in the Constitution, and such implied powers as are necessary and proper to carry into effect the enumerated powers, is categorically true only in respect to our internal affairs. . . . [299 U.S. 315-316, 81 L. Ed. 260, 57 S. Ct. 219.]

> It results that the investment of the federal government with the powers of external sovereignty did not depend upon the affirmative grants of the Constitution. The powers to declare and wage war, to conclude peace, to make treaties, to maintain diplomatic relations with other sovereignties, if they had never been mentioned in the Constitution, would have vested in the federal government as necessary concomitants of nationality. . . . [299 U.S. 318, 81 L. Ed. 261, 57 S. Ct. 220.] the power to make such international agreements as do not constitute treaties in the constitutional sense. . . none

of which is expressly affirmed by the Constitution, nevertheless exist as inherently inseparable from the conception of nationality. *This court recognized, and in each of the cases cited found the warrant for its conclusions not in the provisions of the Constitution, but in the law of nations.* [Italics added. 229 U.S. 318, 81 L. Ed. 262, 57 S. Ct. 220.]

One of the cases cited by Justice Sutherland, above, was *B. Altman & Co. v. United States* (cited and discussed in Note 4), which related to an executive agreement with France on the matter of trade. As indicated in Note 4, Congress had authorized President Theodore Roosevelt in Section 3 of the Tariff Act of 1897 to enter into such agreements. So, the Altman Case did not validate an executive agreement not authorized by Congress, as Justice Sutherland would apparently deceptively mislead us to believe.

Justice George Sutherland's "authority" to ignore the Constitution came from former Senator George Sutherland's *Constitutional Power and World Affairs* (New York: Columbia University Press, 1919, and Johnson Reprint Corp., 1970), pp. 170-171. His "authority" is in the following words from his pen:

In the course of the adventurous voyage upon which we are embarked we have reached the point where we must sail in closer contact with other ships of the fleet. In other words, the period of national detachment has ended and that of international coöperation has supervened. The other nations with whom we shall coöperate will want to know, and will have a right to know, not

21

only the things we think should be included in the new order, but what we are willing and able to do upon our part toward their consummation. We have become too closely and vitally involved in the tangle of international problems to any longer, or ever again, stand apart. It would not only be a great embarrassment, but a great misfortune, if it should transpire that there is anything which we ought but which, for lack of constitutional power, we are able to do. The importance of conceding to the national government the full measure of power which it has been the main purpose of the preceding discussions to sustain, is clearly apparent. The time is fast approaching, if it be not already here, when we must be able to assert and maintain for that government the unimpaired powers of complete external sovereignty. We must not – we cannot – enter upon this field of amplified activity with half-developed limbs. The complete powers of the governments of other nations must be matched by the complete powers of our own government. Upon this enlarged stage of international negotiation and coöperation we cannot afford to play the part of a political cripple. Our government must come to its new tasks not only with full, but with unquestioned powers. To be obliged to confess, when called upon to deal with some novel but vital matter, that the government lacked sufficient authority, because of the absence of affirmative language in the Constitution, would be most humiliating and regrettable; and to find the power only after a microscopic search of that instrument, and a strained or doubtful interpretation of its words, would be almost as unfortunate. Any theory of constitutional construction which leads to such a result will not bear analysis and must be rejected.

I see nothing humiliating or regrettable about requiring the United States Government to act in accord with the United States Constitution. On the contrary, it is humiliating to the People and regrettable for the United States Government to be so arrogant and contemptible as to not act in accord with the United States Constitution. Moreover, for it to not do so is unconstitutional and unlawful.

Since Justice Sutherland already had his mind set to project his prejudices as law in preference to the clearly written Law of the Constitution and since he did not disqualify himself but rather slyly influenced the majority on the matter with his predjudicial and unconstitutional position, the portion of the Curtiss-Wright decision that reflects George Sutherland's unconstitutional bias cannot be used as a precedent. Neither can, for the same reason, *United States* v. *Belmont*, supra, which relied on his bias in the Curtiss-Wright decision for authority and which included his bias. Either George Sutherland's book, which he could not cite but cited inferentially as the "law of nations," is the law or the Constitution is the Law. (The same criteria could be applied to Gunnar Myrdal's books, Marx's books, and other books that have been used to amend the Constitution via the Supreme Court.)

[9]The cited clause follows:

"He shall have Power, by and with the Advice and

Consent of the Senate, to make Treaties, provided two-thirds of the Senators present concur. . ."

[10]Contrary to popular opinion, Chief Justice John Marshall did not say in *Marbury v. Madison*, 1 Cranch 137, 5 U.S. 137, 2 L. Ed. 60 (1803), that the Constitution is what the Supreme Court says it is. He said, among other things, the following:

That the people have an original right to establish, for their future government, such principles, as, in their opinion, shall most conduce to their own happiness is the basis on which the whole American fabric has been erected. . . .

This original and supreme will organizes the government, and assigns to different departments their respective powers. It may either stop here, or establish certain limits not to be transcended by those departments. [1 Cranch 176, 5 U.S. 176, 2 L. Ed. 73.]

The government of the United States is of the latter description. The powers of the legislature are defined and limited; and that those limits may not be mistaken, or forgotten, the constitution is written. To what purpose are powers limited, and to what purpose is that limitation committed to writing, if these limits may, at any time, be passed by those intended to be restrained? The distinction between a government with limited and unlimited powers is abolished, if those limits do not confine the persons on whom they are imposed and if acts prohibited and acts allowed are of equal obligation. It is a proposition too plain to be contested, that

24

the constitution controls any legislative act repugnant to it; or, that the legislature may alter the constitution by an ordinary act. [1 Cranch 176-177, 5 U.S. 176-177, 2 L. Ed. 73.]

Between these alternatives there is no middle ground. The constitution is either a superior paramount law, unchangeable by ordinary means, or it is on a level with ordinary legislative acts, and, like other acts, is alterable when the legislature shall please to alter it.

If the former part of the alternative be true, then a legislative act contrary to the constitution is not law; if the latter part be true, then written constitutions are absurd attempts, on the part of the people, to limit a power in its own nature illimitable. . . .

It is emphatically the province and duty of the judicial department to say what the law is. Those who apply the rule to particular cases, must of necessity expound and interpret that rule. If two laws conflict with each other, the courts must decide on the operation of each. [1 Cranch 177, 5 U.S. 177, 2 L. Ed. 73.]

So if a law be in opposition to the constitution; if both the law and the constitution apply to a particular case, so that the court must either decide that case conformably to the law, disregarding the constitution; or conformably to the constitution, disregarding the law; the court must determine which of these conflicting rules governs the case. This is of the very essence of judicial duty. [1 Cranch 178, 5 U.S. 178, 2 L. Ed.

73-74.]

If, then, the courts are to regard the constitution, and the constitution is superior to any ordinary act of the legislature, the constitution, and not such ordinary act, must govern the case to which they both apply.

Those, then, who controvert the principle that the constitution is to be considered, in court, as paramount law, are reduced to the necessity of maintaining that courts must close their eyes on the constitution, and see only the law.

This doctrine would subvert the very foundation of all written constitutions. It would declare that an act which, according to the principles and theory of our government, is entirely void, is yet, in practice, completely obligatory. . . .

That it thus reduces to nothing what we have deemed the greatest improvement in political institutions, a written constitution, would of itself be sufficient, in America, where written constitutions have been viewed with so much reverence, for rejecting the construction. . . . [1 Cranch 178, 5 U.S. 178, 2 L. Ed. 74.]

From these and from many other selections which might be made, it is apparent, that the framers of the constitution contemplated that instrument as a rule for the government of courts as well as of the legislature. [Italics added. 1 Cranch 179-180, 5 U.S. 179-180, 2 L. Ed. 74.]

Why otherwise does it direct the judges to take an oath to support it?

Why does a judge swear to discharge his

26

duties agreeably to the constitution of the United States, if that constitution forms no rule for his government? . . .

It is also not entirely unworthy of observation, that in declaring what shall be the supreme law of the land, the constitution itself is first mentioned; and not the laws of the United States generally, but those only which shall be made in pursuance of the constitution, have that rank.

Thus, the particular phraseology of the constitution of the United States confirms and strengthens the principle, supposed to be essential to all written constitutions, that a law repugnant to the constitution is void; and that courts, as well as other departments, are bound by that instrument. [Italics added. 1 Cranch 180, 5 U.S. 180, 2 L. Ed. 74.]

Chief Justice John Marshall rolls on, in his prologue to the opinion of the Court in *McCullough v. Maryland*, 4 Wheat. 316, 17 U.S. 316, 4 L. Ed. 579 (1819), as follows

2. The power to establish such a corporation is implied, and involved in the grant for specific powers in the constitution, because the end involves the means necessary to carry it into effect. A power without the means to use it is a nullity. But we are not driven to seek for this power in implication; because the constitution, after enumerating certain specific powers, expressly gives to Congress the power "To make all Laws which shall be necessary and proper for carrying into Execution the foregoing Powers,

27

and all other Powers vested by this Constitution in the Government of the United States, or in any Department or Officer thereof." [Last paragraph, Section 8, Article I, U.S. Constitution.] If, therefore, the act of Congress establishing the bank was necessary and proper to carry into execution any one or more of the enumerated powers, the authority to pass it is expressly delegated to Congress by the constitution. . . . [4 Wheat. 353, 17 U.S. 353, 4 L. Ed. 588.] The convention well knew that it was utterly vain and nugatory to give to Congress certain specific powers, without the means of enforcing those powers. . . . To make a law constitutional, nothing more is necessary than that it should be fairly adapted to carry into effect some specific power given to Congress. . . . [4 Wheat. 356, 17 U.S. 356, 4 L. Ed. 489.] Any government of limited sovereignty can create corporations only with reference to the limited powers that government possesses. [4 Wheat. 358, 17 U.S. 358, 4 L. Ed. 489.]

. . . It is well known, that many of the powers which are expressly granted to the national government in the constitution, were most reluctantly conceded by the people, who were lulled into confidence by the assurances of its advocates, that it contained no latent ambiguity, but was to be limited to the literal terms of the grant; and in order to quiet all alarm, the 10th article of amendments was added, declaring "that the powers not delegated to the United States by the constitution, nor prohibited by it to the States, are reserved to the States respectively, or to the people." It would seem that human language could not furnish words less liable to misconstruction! But it is contended, that the powers expressly granted to the national government in the constitution, are enlarged to an indefinite extent, by the sweeping clause, authorizing Congress to make all laws which shall be necessary and proper for carrying into execution the powers expressly delegated to the national government, or any of its departments or officers. Now, we insist, that this clause shows that the intention of the Convention was to define the powers of government with utmost precision and accuracy. [4 Wheat. 365-366, 17 U.S. 365-366, 4 L. Ed. 591.]

. . . We are now called upon to apply that theory of interpretation which was then rejected by the friends of the new constitution, and we are asked to engraft upon it powers of vast extent, which were disclaimed by them, and which, if they had been fairly avowed at the time, would have prevented its adoption. [4 Wheat. 373, 17 U.S. 373, 4 L. Ed. 593.]

. . . But the constitution acts directly on the people, by means of powers communicated directly from the people. [4 Wheat. 377, 17 U.S. 377, 4 L. Ed. 594.]

In the opinion of the Court itself, Chief Justice Marshall wrote:

. . . No political dreamer was ever wild

enough to think of breaking down the lines which separate the states, and of compounding the American people into one common mass. . . .

From these conventions the constitution derives its whole authority. The government proceeds directly from the people. . . . [4 Wheat. 303, 17 U.S. 403, 4 L. Ed. 601.]

. . . Congress is not empowered by it to make all laws, which may have relation to the powers conferred on the government, but such only as may be "necessary and proper" for carrying them into execution. The word "necessary" is considered as controlling the whole sentence, and as limiting the right to pass laws for the execution of the granted powers, to such laws as are indispensable, and without which the power would be nugatory. [4 Wheat. 413, 17 U.S. 413, 4 L. Ed. 603.]

. . . Let the end be legitimate, let it be within the scope of the constitution, and all means which are appropriate, which are plainly adapted to that end, which are not prohibited, but consist with the letter and spirit of the constitution, are constitutional. [4 Wheat. 421, 17 U.S. 421, 4 L. Ed. 605.]

Chief Justice John Marshall said that the Supreme Court is bound to interpret the Constitution by its literal meaning as adopted, not by gossamer definitions that change shape with the popular winds (an example of which is the redefinition of the General Welfare Clause in *Helvering, Commissioner of Internal Revenue v. Davis*, 301 U.S. 619, 81 L. Ed. 1307, 57 S. Ct. 904 [1937]). Marshall also said that the applications projecting from the implied powers must be consistent with the Constitution. In the above constructions, he put the Shackles of the Constitution on the Supreme Court, the Congress, the Federal Government, and, by projection, on every governmental body in the country; and he said, in effect, "No nonsense. The Constitution is the Law."

John Marshall summarized it all in his dissenting opinion in *Ogden v. Saunders*, 12 Wheat. 213, 25 U.S. 213, 6 L. Ed. 606 (1827), as follows:

> . . . To say that the intention of the instrument must prevail; that this intention must be collected from its words; that its words are to be understood in that sense in which they are generally used by those for whom the instrument was intended; that its provisions are neither to be restricted into insignificence, nor extended to objects not comprehended in them nor contemplated by its framers is to repeat what has been already said at large, and is all that can be necessary. [12 Wheat. 332, 25 U.S. 332, 6 L. Ed. 647.]

[11]Hamilton, Madison, and Jay followed up the Constitutional Convention with *The Federalist Papers*, to deal with the formation of public opinion in support of ratification of the Constitution by the State Legislatures; and in the process they necessarily elaborated on the Constitution, which inevitably had the effect of further explaining the meaning of its provisions. By cross-referencing from the Constitution to *The Federalist Papers* and *vice-versa*, it is difficult indeed to misinterpret most of its provisions. (Alexander Hamilton, James Madison, and John Jay, *The*

Federalist Papers, annot. Clinton Rossiter [New York; and Scarborough, Ontario, Canada: The New American Library, Inc.; London: The New English Library, Ltd., 1961].)

An incisive essay on understanding the Constitution and interpreting it in terms of the spirit and intent of the Framers is Edward J. Erler's "The Constitution of Principle," *Still the Law of the Land?* (Hillsdale, Michigan: Hillsdale College Press, 1987), p. 15.

Another helpful essay is Stephen J. Markman's "The Jurisprudence of Constitutional Amendments," *ibid.*, p. 79.

[12]Perhaps we should clean up the Supreme Court's mud puddle on treaties and executive agreements, by adopting to the Constitution a modification of the Bricker Amendment (U.S. Cong., 2nd sess., 1952, 98, pt. 1: 908; and S.J. Res. 1, 83rd Cong., 1st sess.). A modified Bricker Amendment follows:

Section 1. No treaty or executive agreement shall be made respecting the rights of citizens of the United States protected by this Constitution or abridging or prohibiting the free exercise thereof.

Section 2. No treaty or executive agreement shall vest in any international organization or in any foreign power any of the legislative, executive, or judicial powers vested by this Constitution in the Congress, the President, and in the courts of the United States, respectively.

Section 3. Executive agreements with foreign powers not consented to by two-thirds of the Senate present or preauthorized by Congress, with the majority in the Senate being two-thirds of the Senate present, shall not have the power of a treaty, as described in Paragraph 2, Article VI, of this Constitution.

Section 4. The President shall publish all executive agreements, except those which in his judgment require secrecy shall be submitted to appropriate committees of the Congress in lieu of publication.

Section 5. The Congress shall have the power to enforce this article by appropriate legislation.

Section 6. No legislation by the Congress to implement a treaty or properly consented to or preauthorized executive agreement shall be valid, if such legislation is contrary to or in excess of the powers delegated to the Congress by the Constitution.

Section 7. This article shall be inoperative, unless it shall have been ratified as an amendment to the Constitution by the legislatures of three-fourths of the several States within seven years from the date of its submission.

[13] We might consider adopting as a general rule the following:

> In asserting our constitutional rights, we have the aid of a principle which has perhaps never been openly advanced, but which is none the less obviously valid: the doctrine of *stare decisis* cannot be constitutionally invoked in the decision of constitutional questions. The Constitution of the United States, to take the leading example of a written constitition, is, by essential nature and by express terms, . . . the supreme law of the land. [United States Constitution, Article VI, Clause 2.] When, therefore, the United States Supreme Court misinterprets its provisions, it is still the Constitition which is the law, and not the decision of the court. Any other doctrine would make it possible for the court, through

a series of adjudications gradually and insidiously encroaching upon the terms of the original instrument, to pervert its meaning and eventually to abrogate the Constitution in its entirety. [This is precisely what has been happening.] Any other doctrine would make it possible for the executive and legislative branches of the government to subvert the court to its own desires and by its aid to nullify the guaranties of public safety. [Ditto.] The only protection which we can have against these results is to hold the court itself rigorously to the terms of the Constitution, to subject all its decisions to the unyielding test of reason, and, when any one of them fails to find a rational support in the Constitution, to recognize that it is not the law of the land. Any citizen, therefore, whose liberty or property is at stake, has an absolute constitutional right to appear before the court and challenge its interpretations of the Constitution, no matter how often they have been promulgated, upon the ground that they are repugnant to its provisions. In other words, he has a constitutional right to assert before the court itself that its decisions are themselves unconstitutional, and if he can establish his assertion, the court is under a sworn duty to reverse itself, because it is under a sworn duty to uphold the Constitution rather than its own opinions.

When the bar of our country understands this and respectfully but inexorably requires of the Supreme Court that it shall continually justify its decisions by the Constitution and not by its own precedents, we shall attain a new conception of the power of our constitutional guaranties. [Everett V. Abbot, *Justice and the Modern Law* (Boston and New York: Houghton Mifflin Co., 1913), pp. 76-78.]

[14]Further details on the critical issues that are discussed in this essay are covered in V. Orval Watts' concise report, *United Nations: Planned Tyranny* (New York: Devin-Adair Co., 1955).

Pertinent to the discussion are many parts of William J. Palmer's brief essay, *The Court -vs- the People* (Chicago: Chas. Hallberg & Co., 1969).

For information on what some of the Founders said about treaties, one should refer to the index of *The Federalist Papers*, Hamilton, Madison, and Jay. (Any serious study of the Constitution should include a careful reading of *The Federalist Papers*. It is more efficient to work with an edition that has a copy of the Constitution, with annotations in the margins to *The Federalist Papers*.)

A concise explanation of natural law can be found in Murray N. Rothbard's *The Ethics of Liberty* (Atlantic Highlands, New Jersey: Humanities Press, Inc., 1982), pp. 1-26.

The General Welfare Clause[1]

George W. Nilsson

The Constitution of Vermont reminds us:

". . . That frequent recurrence to fundamental principles, and a firm adherence to justice, moderation, temperance, industry and frugality, are absolutely necessary to preserve the blessings of liberty and keep government free. . . ."[2]

In addition to the threats of danger from outside of the United States and subversion within, the constitutional republic of the United States is being threatened by the concentration of power in the Federal Government, in spite of and contrary to the "checks and balances" of the Constitution.

Much of such concentration has been due to two World Wars and the Korean War; but, more especially, it has been caused by twisting out of shape the Interstate Commerce Clause of the Constitution (Article I, Section 8, Clause 3), by using taxing power for punitive purposes instead of for raising revenue as authorized, and by misusing the General Welfare Clause.

More and more power is being seized by or surrendered to the Federal Government under the guise of the alleged grant of power in the General Welfare Clause of the Constitution (Article I, Section 8, Clause 1), which follows:

37

". . . The Congress shall have the Power To lay and collect Taxes, Duties, Imposts and Excises, to pay the Debts and provide for the common Defence and general Welfare of the United States. . . ."

This clause is followed by sixteen other clauses specifying the various powers of Congress, such as the power to borrow money (Clause 2), the power to regulate foreign and interstate commerce (Clause 3), etc. Then Clause 18 gives the Congress power, as follows: "To make all Laws which shall be necessary and proper for carrying into Execution the foregoing Powers. . . ." This last clause would have been unnecessary if Clause 1 gave "general welfare power."

For 140 years it was generally recognized that the quotation from Clause 1 was not a grant of "general welfare power." Many Presidents vetoed acts passed by Congress for that reason. President Andrew Jackson vetoed the Maysville Road Bill on May 27, 1930, on that ground.[3]

In the 1930's the Supreme Court "discovered" that the clause granted "general welfare power," and more and more this has been used to pass legislation based solely on this alleged grant of general welfare power. . . .

Rules for Interpretation

There is a general rule of law that holds, as follows: When the statement of a general proposition is followed by specific provision, the specific provisions prevail. This rule is stated by James Madison in *The Federalist Papers*, Number 41,[4] and by Alexander Hamilton in *The Federalist Papers*, Number 83.[5] It is applied by Justice

Joseph Story to Article I, Section 8, enumerating the powers of Congress, in Sections 909-911 of his *Commentaries on the Constitution of the United States*.[6] He shows that the specific powers enumerated in Clauses 2 through 7 limit Clause 1, which refers to general welfare. In Section 910, page 632, he wrote as follows:

> . . . Nothing is more natural or common, than first to use a general phrase, and then to qualify it by a recital of particulars. But the idea of an enumeration of particulars, which neither explain, nor qualify the general meaning, and can have no other effect, than to confound and mislead, is an absurdity, which no one ought to charge on the enlightened authors of the constitution. . . . It would be to charge them either with premediated folly, or premeditated fraud.

Another yardstick, which is discussed below, that one can use in determining the meaning of the General Welfare Clause is that the powers delegated to the United States by the Constitution are few, defined, and limited. Justice Felix Frankfurter projected that rule in the "Opinion of the Court" in *Polish National Alliance of the United States of North America v. National Labor Relations Board*, 332 U.S. 643, 88 L. Ed. 1509, 64 S. Ct. 1196 (1944), as follows:

> The interpenetrations of modern society have not wiped out state lines. It is not for us to make inroads upon our federal system either by indifference to its maintenance or excessive regard for the unifying forces of modern technology. Scholastic reasoning may prove that no activity is isolated within the boundaries of a

single State, but that cannot justify absorption of legislative power by the United States over every activity. [322 U.S. 650, 88 L. Ed. 1516, 64 S. Ct. 1200.]

Common Sense and Logic—
Climate of Opinion in 1787

In 1787 when the Constitution was adopted, the Colonists had been through eight years of war and four years of "a critical period." Knowing what led up to the war and reading the charges in the Declaration of Independence, can anyone for a minute think that the Colonists generally and the members of the Constitutional Convention specifically would have adopted a Constitution which granted general welfare powers to the Federal Government?

The resistance to the adoption of the Constitution, which will be discussed hereafter, shows what the people generally felt.

This is summarized by Albert J. Beveridge in his great biography, *The Life of John Marshall*. In writing about the convention called in the State of Virginia for the purpose of discussing the ratification of the proposed United States Constitution, he described the parliamentary strength of the delegates against the adoption of the Constitution in relation to the general feeling of the people against a strong central government in these words:

They had on their side the fears of the people, who, as has appeared, looked on all government with suspicion, on any vital government with hostility, and on a great central Government as some distant and monstrous thing, too far away to be within their reach, too powerful to be resisted, too high and exalted for the good of the common man, too dangerous to be tried. It was, to the masses, something new, vague, and awful; something to oppress the poor, the weak, the debtor, the settler; something to strengthen and enrich the already strong and opulent, the merchant, the creditor, the financial interests.

True, the people had suffered by the loose arrangement under which they now lived; but, after all, had not they and their "liberties" survived? And surely they would suffer even more, they felt, under this stronger power; but would they and their "liberties" survive its "oppression"? They thought not.[7]

Thomas Jefferson made the same point in 1823, as follows:

I have been blamed for saying that a prevalence of the doctrine of consolidation would one day call for reformation or revolution. *I answer by asking if a single State of the Union would have agreed to the Constitution had it given all powers to the General Government? If the whole opposition to it did not proceed from the jealousy and fear of every State of being subjected to the other States in matters merely its own?* [Italics added.] And if there is any reason to believe the States more disposed now than then to acquiesce in this general surrender of all

their rights and powers to a consolidated government, one and undivided?[8]

On Febraury 16, 1783, four years before the Constitutional Convention, Pelatiah Webster published a pam-
phlet containing his idea of a proposed constitution for the
United States. The whole draft can be found in Hannis
Taylor's *The Origin and Growth of the American Constitution*,[9] An appendix beginning at page 527. On page
542 is Paragraph 7 of his proposed constitution. In it,
Webster wrote:

> I propose further that the powers of Con-
> gress, and all other departments acting under
> them, shall all be restricted to such matters only
> of *general necessity and utility to all the States
> as cannot come within the jurisdiction of any par-
> ticular State, or to which the authority of any par-
> ticular State is not competent,* so that each par-
> ticular State shall enjoy all sovereignty and
> supreme authority to all intents and purposes,
> excepting only those high authorities and powers
> by them delegated to Congress for the purposes
> of the general union. [Italics added.]

Articles of Confederation

Article VIII of the Articles of Confederation begins with
the following language:

"All charges of war, and all other expences that shall
be incurred for the common defence or general
welfare. . . ."[10]

James Madison pointed out in a letter to Edmund

Pendleton, dated January 21, 1792, that the "general welfare clause" had been copied from the Articles of Confederation, and then wrote:

> . . . where it was always understood as nothing more than a general caption to the specified powers, and it is a fact that it was preferred in the new instrument for that very reason as less than any other to misconstruction.[11]

Debates in the Federal Convention

A summary of the day-to-day proceedings of the Constitutional Convention of 1787 is found in Charles Warren's *The Making of the Constitution*.[12]

From a study of the records of the Convention, it will appear that from time to time efforts were made by some delegates to have the Constitution grant broad general powers to the Federal Government. Each time such a proposal was advanced, it was rejected.

Beginning on page 464 of Warren's work is a discussion of the taxing power and the General Welfare Clause, as follows:

> It is equally clear that no delegate, at that time, conceived that the phraseology recommended by the Committee was, in any way, altering or expanding the *power* to levy taxes which had theretofore been voted, except to extend the application of that power to these prior debts. The whole intent of the change was evidently to make the power to levy taxes for the purpose of paying these debts an *express* power,

instead of leaving it to be *implied* or doubtful. The question arises: Why, then, did the Committee insert the additional words, "and provide for the common Defence and general Welfare of the United States"? The probable reason for their insertion by Judge Brearley's Committee was as follows. . . . Had the Convention simply voted that Congress should have "power to lay and collect taxes, duties, imposts and excises to *pay the debts of* the United States," and had it stopped there, such a provision might have been construed as giving Congress the power to levy and collect taxes to pay the old debts and only [to tax] for that purpose. Some words evidently had to be added that would make clear the power of Congress to levy taxes for all the National purposes set forth in the grants of power subsequently specified in this section. Evidently the Committee selected these words, "to provide for the general Welfare," as comprising all the other purposes for which Congress was to be empowered to levy and collect taxes. They selected these words as embracing all the subsequent limited grants of power which the Committee of Detail, in its Report of August 6, had specified as constituting that amount of common defense and general welfare which the National Government ought to control and as to which it ought to have power of legislation. In other words, the phrase, "to provide for the general Welfare," is merely a general description of the amount of welfare which was to be accomplished by carrying out those enumerated and limited powers vested in Congress – and no others.

Debates in the Various States for the Adoption of the Constitution

History tells us that in 1787 there was great opposition to the adoption of the proposed new Constitution. As a matter of fact, it squeaked through by a very few votes in a number of States. Only on the condition that a Bill of Rights be added, it was ratified by Massachusetts 187 to 168, by Virginia 89 to 79, and by New York 30 to 27.

The Federalist Papers were written by Alexander Hamilton, James Madison, and John Jay in support of the adoption of the Constitution, principally in connection with the debates in New York, where there was strong opposition to the Constitution.

In *The Federalist Papers*, Number 41, James Madison (after pointing out the objections to the clause, ". . . to lay and collect Taxes. . . for the. . . general Welfare. . ."), wrote:

> But what color can the objection have, when a specification of the objects alluded to by these general terms immediately follows and is not even separated by a longer pause than a semicolon? If the different parts of the same instrument ought to be so expounded as to give meaning to every part which will bear it, shall one part of the same sentence be excluded altogether from a share in the meaning; and shall the more doubtful and

45

indefinite terms be retained in their full extent, and the clear and precise expressions be denied any signification whatsoever? For what purpose could the enumeration of particular powers be inserted, if these and all others were meant to be included in the preceding general power? Nothing is more natural nor common than first to use a general phrase, and then to explain and qualify it by a recital of particulars.[13]

Federal Government Given
Only Limited Powers

In considering the question of whether or not this "general welfare" clause (Article I, Section 8, Clause 1), is a grant of power, we must also remember that the powers granted to the Federal Government were few and defined. James Madison, in *The Federalist Papers*, Number 45, wrote:

The powers delegated by the proposed Constitution to the federal government are few and defined. Those which are to remain in the State governments are numerous and indefinite. The former will be exercised principally on external objects, as war, peace, negotiation, and foreign commerce; with which last the power of taxation will, for the most part, be connected. The powers reserved to the several States will extend to all the objects which, in the ordinary course of affairs, concern the lives, liberties, and properties of the people, and the internal order, improvement, and prosperity of the State.[14]

Alexander Hamilton, himself, who argued in the Constitutional Convention for general instead of particular enumeration of powers, nevertheless wrote in *The Federalist Papers*, Number 83:

> . . . The plan of the convention declares that the power of Congress, or, in other words, of the *national legislature,* shall extend to certain enumerated cases. This specification of particulars evidently excludes all pretension to a general legislative authority, because an affirmative grant of special powers would be absurd, as well as useless, if a general authority was intended.[15]

Since the people were persuaded to adopt the Constitution on the basis that the Federal Government was being given only limited and specified powers, how dare anyone, in good conscience, now take the position that the words, "general welfare," give the Federal Government unlimited power?

This principle was restated by Franklin D. Roosevelt on March 2, 1930, while he was Governor of New York, in a speech which was entitled, "An Address on the State Rights,"[16] He said in part:

> "The preservation of this "Home Rule" by the States is not a cry of jealous Commonwealths seeking their own aggrandizement at the expense of sister States. It is a fundamental necessity if we are to remain a truly united country. . . . [P. 570.]

Now, to bring about government by oligarchy masquerading as democracy, it is fundamentally essential that practically all authority and control be centralized in our National Government. The individual sovereignty of our States must first be destroyed, except in mere minor matters of legislation. We are safe from the danger of any such departure from the principles on which this country was founded just as long as the individual home rule of the States is scrupulously preserved and fought for whenever it seems in danger. [Pp. 571-572.]

Thus it will be seen that this "Home Rule" is a most important thing, a most vital thing, if we are to continue along the course on which we have so far progressed with such unprecedented success. [P. 572.]

The Effect of the Bill of Rights

In many of the States, the Constitution was adopted only when it was accompanied by a resolution demanding that a Bill of Rights be added to the Constitution. If the people of the various States were satisfied with the Constitution as written, they certainly would not have demanded the added protection of the Bill of Rights.

As pointed out under the above centerhead, "Common Sense and Logic – Climate of Opinion in 1787," certainly no State would have adopted the Constitution if the Congress had been given *carte blanche* to pass any law or do anything which it desired or which it felt was for the "general welfare."

This demand for a Bill of Rights, therefore should be sufficient to prove that the Constitution, and particularly Article I, Section 8, Clause 1, did not grant general welfare power to the Federal Government.

True to his promise, James Madison, in the First Congress, which met in 1789, caused to be passed a Bill of Rights containing twelve sections, ten of which were adopted and went into effect on December 15, 1791.

This Bill of Rights and particularly the Ninth and Tenth Amendments are further and conclusive proof that the clause that we are discussing did not grant any authority to the Federal Government to pass any laws based on "general welfare powers."

Statements by Contemporaries after

Adoption of the Constitution

On December 5, 1791, Secretary of the Treasury Alexander Hamilton presented to the Congress his "Report on Manufactures."

Madison delivered an address in Congress against the Report, in which he said in part:

> If Congress can apply money indefinitely to the general welfare, and are the sole and supreme judges of the general welfare, they may take the care of religion into their own hands; they may establish teachers in every State, county, and parish, and pay them out of the public Treasury; they may take into their own hands the education of children, establishing in like man-

ner schools throughout the Union; they may undertake the regulation of all roads, other than post roads. In short, everything, from the highest object of State legislation, down to the most minute object of police, would be thrown under the power of Congress; for every object I have mentioned would admit the application of money, visions for the general welfare."[17]

The Report was pigeonholed, the first major defeat for one of Hamilton's most cherished policies.

Moreover, on the same question, James Madison, on January 1, 1792, in a letter to Henry Lee, Governor of Virginia, said in part:

> . . . What think you of the commentary. . . on the terms "general welfare"? – The federal government has been hitherto limited to the specified powers, by the Greatest Champions for Latitude in expounding those power – If not only the *means*, but the objects are unlimited, the parchment had better be thrown into the fire at once.[18]

In a letter to Edmund Pendleton on January 21, 1792, Madison wrote:

> . . . If Congress can do whatever in their *discretion* can be *done by money*, and will promote the *general welfare*, the government is no longer one possessing enumerated powers, but an indefinite one subject to particular exceptions.[19]

Thomas Jefferson had the same views. He wrote to Albert Gallatin in 1817, about the General Welfare Clause, in which letter he wrote:

You will have learned that an act for internal improvement, after passing both Houses, was negatived by the President. The act was founded, avowedly, on the principle that the phrase in the Constitution which authorizes Congress "to lay taxes, to pay the debts and provide for the general welfare," was an *extension* of the powers *specifically enumerated* to whatever would promote the general welfare; and this, you know, was the Federal doctrine. Whereas our tenet ever was, and, indeed, it is almost the only landmark which now divides the Federalists and the Republicans, that Congress had not unlimited powers to provide for the general welfare, but was *restrained to those specifically enumerated*; and that, as it was never meant that they should provide for that welfare but by the exercise of the enumerated powers, so it could not have meant that they should *raise money for purposes which the enumeration did not place under their action*; consequently, that the *specification* of powers *is a limitation* on the purposes for which they may raise money.[20]

Abraham Baldwin, a member of the Constitutional Convention, said in Congress in 1798 the following:

". . . to provide for the common Defence and general Welfare" had "never been considered as a source of legislative power, as it is only a member introduced to *limit* the other parts of the sentence."[21]

Conclusion

To say that these modern ideas of "general welfare power" are those of Alexander Hamilton is to malign him. Alexander Hamilton was a great patriot and statesman. His ideas of a new government were far different from those embodied in the Constitution, but after the Constitution was adopted, he faithfully and enthusiastically supported it. For instance, he wrote most of *The Federalist Papers*.

Even though Alexander Hamilton had espoused such ideas as are now ascribed to him, such ideas were not accepted as part of the Constitution as finally adopted and, therefore, must not be used to interpret the Constitution.

Since Alexander Hamilton's views were rejected by the Constitutional Convention of 1787 (not even being referred to a committee,[22] since Alexander Hamilton was absent from the Convention about one-half of the time (once from June 29 to the middle of August, 1787), and since his views against the inclusion of a Bill of Rights were rejected, the idea that his views are now being accepted is a clear acknowledgement that the spirit and letter of the Constitution as written are now being perverted.

It is therefore clear from history, common sense, the records of the Constitutional Convention, *The Federalist Papers*, the debates in the ratification Conventions in the States, and precedents followed for more than 140 years that *there is no grant of general welfare power in the Constitution of the United States.*

Although it would seen that such general welfare power is not needed [and is economically, psychologically, and politically unsound], the amending clause of the

Constitution should be followed [rather than permit the Supreme Court to sit unconstitutionally as a constitutional convention], if it should be determined that it is necessary.

The dire results of undermining the Constitution were pointed out by Daniel Webster in his eulogy of George Washington in 1832, in which he said in part:

Other misfortunes may be borne, or their effects overcome. . . .

But who shall reconstruct the fabric of demolished Government? Who shall rear again the well-proportioned columns of constitutional liberty? [Italics added.] Who shall frame together the skillful architecture which unites national sovereignty with State rights, individual security and public prosperity?[23]

Every lawyer, when he or she is admitted to the Bar, takes an oath to "uphold, defend, and protect the Constitution of the Unites Sates." The same oath is taken by practically all judges, elected office holders, and numerous politically appointed officials. Military officers take the oath. Even many private clubs and lodges require this oath of its members and officers.

Since the Constitution is being ignored, misconstrued, and circumvented by legislation, by court decisions, and by executive action, it is time that the fundamental principles of the Constitution be reexamined by every concerned citizen, lawyer, judge, elected office holder, and appointed office holder and that each take his or her responsibility in an Ideological Crusade to reestablish the principles and the spirit of the Declaration of Independence, the Constitution, and the Bill of Rights.[24]

Notes

[1]This essay originally appeared in the *American Bar Association Journal*, XLVII (January, 1961), 43. The original title is "There Is No 'General Welfare Power' in the Constitution of the United States."

[2]Constitution of Vermont, Part First, Article XVIII.

[3]James D. Richardson, comp., *A Compilation of the Messages and Papers of the Presidents* (New York: Bureau of National Literature, Inc., 1897), III, 1046-1056.

[4]Alexander Hamilton, James Madison, and John Jay, *The Federalist Papers*, annot. Clinton Rossiter (New York; and Scarborough, Ontario, Canada: The New American Library, Inc.; London: The New English Library, Ltd., 1961), p. 263. Quotation is in text above under centerhead, "Federal Government Given Only Limited Powers."

[5]*Ibid.*, p. 497. Quotation is in text above under centerhead, "Federal Government Given Only Limited Powers."

[6]Joseph Story, *Commentaries on the Constitution of the United States* (2nd ed.; Boston: Charles C. Little and James Brown, 1851), I, 631-633.

[7]Albert J. Beveridge, *The Life of John Marshall* (Boston and New York: Houghton Mifflin Co., 1919), I, 371-372.

[8]Thomas James Norton, *Undermining the Constitution: A History of Lawless Government* (New York: The Devin-Adair Co., 1950), p. 192.

[9]Hannis Taylor, *The Origin and Growth of the American Constitution* (Boston and New York: Houghton Mifflin Co., 1911).

[10]Henry Steele Commager (ed.), *Documents of American History* (9th ed.; Englewood Cliffs, New Jersey: Prentice-Hall, Inc., 1973), I, 113.

[11]Adrienne Koch, *Jefferson and Madison: the Great Collaboration* (New York: Oxford University Press, 1964), pp. 128-129.

[12]Charles Warren, *The Making of the Constitution* (New York: Barnes & Noble, Inc., 1967).

[13]Hamilton, Madison, and Jay, *op. cit.*, p. 263.

[14]*Ibid.*, pp. 292-293.

[15]*Ibid.*, p. 497.

[16]*The Public Papers and Addresses of Franklin D. Roosevelt* (New York: Random House, 1938), I.

[17]Koch, *op. cit.* p. 129.

[18]*Ibid.*, p. 128.

[19]*Ibid.*

[20]Norton, *op. cit.*, p. 191.

[21]*Ibid.*, p. 189.

[22]Taylor, *op. cit.*, p. 200.

[23]*The Great Speeches and Orations of Daniel Webster* (Boston: Little, Brown, & Co., 1899), p. 346.

[24]This study should begin with a thorough research and understanding of *The Federalist Papers*. JEN.

Government by Decree through Executive Agreement[1]

Joseph L. Call

. . . The spirit of American institutions is opposed to reposing arbitrary power anywhere. We
have no place in our policy for an omnipotent
leader or body of supreme administrators with
infallible hunches, guided by a super superman
at the head of an absolute hierarchy.[2]

Pursuant to this basic idea, the Standing Committee
on Peace and Law of the American Bar Association has
recommended to the American Bar Association an amendment to the Constitution of the United States to curb the
use of executive agreements by the President (infra, Note
13).

It may generally be stated that an *executive agreement* is an agreement or a covenant[3] that is entered into
between the President of the United States and another
foreign power or country *without* the same having been
submitted to or approved by two-thirds of the Senate present and that may either (1) deal with the international
policies of the two countries or (2) deal with the internal
affairs of the United States or the States therein.[4]

On the other hand it may be stated that a *treaty* is
an agreement or a covenant made by the President of the

57

United States with another foreign power or country and may either (1) deal with the international policies of the two countries or (2) deal with the internal affairs of the United States or the States thereof; but it should be stated that said treaty under the Constitution must be made by the President by and with the *advice* and *consent* of two-thirds of the Senate present.[5]

To be noted at this time is the fact that, while constitutional landmarks have fallen with the judicial sanction and augmentation during the last thirty years,[6] probably the most serious deviation from the constitutional restraints and prohibitions is the power assumed and being assumed with increasing celerity by the Executive branch of the government in the making of executive agreements.

The Law of the People

Comprehensive analysis of executive agreements must be presupposed by a comprehensive knowledge of the fundamentals of American constitutional government. Under the United States Constitution, the Federal Government with its three departments (Legislative, Executive, and Judicial), exists *only* by reason of specific grants of power delegated by the people through the Federal Constitution to the Federal Government. The Federal Government in this country is predicated upon the underlying principle that sovereignty vests in the people[7] and not in the Federal Government or in the State Government or in those executive officers sworn to enforce the duties of the state and that "The powers not delegated to the United States by the Constitution, nor prohibited by it to the States,

are reserved to the States respectively, or to the people."[8]
These cardinal principles are clearly stated by the court in
the case of *Kansas* v. *Colorado* (infra, note 7), in which
the court said:

> . . . But the proposition that there are
> legislative powers affecting the Nation as a whole
> which belong to, although not expressed in the
> grant of powers, is in direct conflict with the doc-
> trine that this is a government of enumerated
> powers. That this is such a government clearly
> appears from the Constitution, independently of
> the Amendments, for otherwise there would be
> an instrument granting certain specified things
> made operative to grant other and distinct things.
> This natural construction of the original body of
> the Constitution is made absolutely certain by the
> Tenth Amendment. This amendment, which was
> seemingly adopted with prescience of just such
> contention as the present, disclosed and
> widespread fear that the National Government
> might, under the pressure of a supposed general
> welfare, attempt to exercise powers which had
> not been granted. [206 U.S. 89-90, 51 L. Ed.
> 971, 27 S. Ct. 664.]

A Dangerous Trend

Since the creation of the Republic there have been
considerably in excess of nine hundred executive
agreements entered into, and the trend, as in all unlawful
usurpation of power, has been to the enlargement of these

unlawfully assumed executive powers.[9] John Marshall, in 1779, as a member of the House of Representatives, declared that "The President is the sole organ of the nation in its external relations, and its sole representative with foreign nations."[10] Based upon this generalized assumption, the practice was started, at least one hundred and fifty years ago, to permit a President to enter into executive agreements with foreign governments on *specified matters, but with Congressional authorization.*[11]

But as in all cases where power is extraconstitutionally assumed, even though naive in its creation, the trend and the ultimate conclusion is one of absolutism. Power is insatiable and if left unchecked will create what it wishes.

> . . . Innovation is dangerous. One incroachment leads to another; precedent gives birth to precedent; what has been done may be done again; thus radical principles are generally broken in upon, and the constitution eventually destroyed. [*Vanhorne's Lessee v. Dorrance*, 2 Dallas 394-395, 2 U.S. 311-312, 1 L. Ed. 394-395 (1795).]

The naive executive agreements authorized by Congress at the inception of the Republic have now mushroomed into a situation in which the right to make executive agreements on *external and internal affairs* has been assumed as a matter of absolute right by the Executive Department of the United States for many years. Such powers, innocuous at the time of their assumption, during the history of the Republic have been asserted by the Executive Department upon matters refused confirmation by the United States Senate;[12] and at the present time these usurpations have assumed such magnitude that the

American form of government, the Constitution, and the American way of life are on the threshold of vitiation.[13]

The Constitution Prevails

To be borne in mind also is the fact that the fundamental law of the land still exists, as expressed in the grant of powers in the Federal Constitution. The repetitious affirmance of the unlawful assumption of rights or powers by the Executive Department and the affirmance of this extraconstitutional assumption of powers by the United States Supreme Court still does not create or make lawful such powers as assumed; nor does the further fact that the making of executive agreements or covenants by the Executive Department of this government has become a practice lend to its constitutional validity.

Such construction is the law regardless of its unconstitutionality in fact. In other words, a differently constituted court may reverse such decisions and return to the Constitution. Charles Warren expressed this principle very clearly when he wrote:

> One other duty toward the Court and towards the public is owed by counsel which should be unflinchingly performed, namely, to insist that the doctrine of *stare decisis* can never be applied to decisions upon constitutional questions. However the Court may interpret the provisions of the Constitution, it is still the Constitution which is the law and not the decision of the Court.[14]

In other words, as pointed out by Patterson, there is

clearly such a thing as an unconstitutional decision of the Supreme Court; but, like an unconstitutional act of Congress, before the act has been declared unconstitutional, it has the force of law, until it is reversed by the court or repealed by a constitutional amendment.[15]

One Source of

Extraconstitutional Decisions

Unfortunately, such decisions result sometimes from political appointments to the Supreme Court and stem not from legal but from partisan opinions or otherwise. Ernest Bates expressed this situation thusly:

> . . . It is a pleasant theory still held by the naive that the President of the United States in making his appointments to the Supreme Court is governed primarily by considerations of merit. That unfortunately has never been the case in the past and is not likely to be the case in the future.[16]

Contrary Points of View

On what possible basis can the proponents of such powers justify their assumption and their execution? The answer actually is that the making of such executive agreements has been consumated without constitutional authorization and that the making has therefore become a *fait accompli* and that thereafter justification is sought for the improper and unlawful execution of the agreement.

In defense of these unlawful assumptions of power, it has been contended that the Framers of the Constitution contemplated distinction between the word, "treaty," and the words, "agreement" or "compact"; that inasmuch as the opening clause of Article II of the Federal Constitution states that "The *executive Power* shall be vested in a President of the United States. . ." (italics added by author); and that – if the word, "treaty," is eliminated in the making of an international agreement and the words, "executive agreement" or "compact," are used in lieu thereof – the President thereby may properly make such an agreement, because of the fact that, since it is not designated as a treaty and consequently does not require the consent of two-thirds of the Senate present, his sole making of it is a valid exercise of his executive power.[17]

Such contention, however, is but a sophistry, a specious and fallacious reasoning, and a play on words. It need only be stated in answering this contention that the statement, "The executive Power shall be vested in a President of the United States," is in no sense a delegation of specific powers or rights but is a generalized statement only in the abstract; it authorizes no affirmative acts, grants no affirmative powers, and authorizes no affirmative action. What meaning it carries must be construed with and analyzed with "those qualifications which naturally result from the other powers granted by that instrument, so that the whole may be interpreted by the spirit which vivifies, and not by the letter which killeth."[18]

It follows, since this ground of reasoning is so obviously a non sequitor, that no further reasoning is necessary.

The further ground for the validity of such executive

63

agreements is to be found in the doctrine of "inherent external sovereignty," of which former Senator Sutherland[19] and later a Justice of the United States Supreme Court was probably one of the most outspoken proponents.

This doctrine advocates that the power to make executive agreements and treaties is derived not only from the power expressly conferred by the Constitution but is also possessed by the Government independent of and as an attribute of sovereignty.[20] In substantiation of this view, Sutherland wrote:

> The time is fast approaching, if it be not already here, when we must be able to assert and maintain for that government the unimpaired powers of complete external sovereignty. . . . The complete powers of the governments of other nations must be matched by the complete powers of our own government. . . . To be obliged to confess, when called upon to deal with some novel but vital matter, that the government lacked sufficient authority. . . would be most humiliating and regrettable. . . .[21]

This view, as expressed by Sutherland in his text in 1919, has been in no wise revised, as respects his views expressed while a member of the Supreme bench. In 1936 in the case of *United States v. Curtiss-Wright Corporation*,[22] he stated – in discussing the doctrine of inherent sovereignty, in a defense of this doctrine, and in an attempt to evade the direct mandates of the Constitution – the following principles:

> . . . The broad statement that the federal government can exercise no powers except those specifically enumerated in the Constitution, and

such implied powers as are necessary and proper to carry into effect the enumerated powers, is categorically true only in respect of our internal affairs. [299 U.S. 315-316, 81 L. Ed. 260, 57 S. Ct. 219.] In that field, the primary purpose of the Constitution was to carve from the general mass of legislative powers *then possessed by the states* such portions as it was thought desirable to vest in the Federal government, leaving those not included in the enumeration still in the states. . . . That this doctrine applies only to powers which the states had, is self-evident. And since the states severally never possessed international powers, such powers could not have been carved from the mass of state powers but obviously were transmitted to the United States from some other source. . . . [299 U.S. 316, 81 L. Ed. 260, 57 S. Ct. 219.]

As a result of the separation from Great Britain by the colonies, acting as a unit, the powers of external sovereignty passed from the Crown not to the colonies severally, but to the colonies in their collective and corporate capacity as the United States of America. [299 U.S. 316, 81 L. Ed. 261, 57 S. Ct. 219.]

It results that the investment of the Federal government with the powers of external sovereignty did not depend upon the affirmative grants of the Constitution. The powers to declare and wage war, to conclude peace, to make treaties, to maintain diplomatic relations with other sovereignties, if they had never mentioned in the Constitution, would have vested in the federal government as necessary concomitants of nationality. [299 U.S. 318, 81 L. Ed. 261, 57 S. Ct. 220.] . . . the power to make such international agreements as do not constitute treaties in the constitutional sense. . . none of which is expressly affirmed by the Constitution, nevertheless exist as inherently inseparable from the conception of nationality. This the court recognized, and in each of the cases cited found the warrant for its conclusions not in the provisions of the Constitution but in the law of nations. [299 U.S. 318, 81 L. Ed. 262, 57 S. Ct. 220.]

History Refutes Sutherland

First of all, the conclusion of Justice Sutherland to the effect that the separation of the thirteen original colonies from Great Britain resulted in the powers of external sovereignty passing from the Crown, not to the colonies severally but to the colonies in an allegedly corporate capacity, is without historical foundation and not in accordance with the history of the Republic. There is nothing farther from historical fact than the proposition that "external sovereignty" passed from the Crown to the colonies in their *collective and corporate capacity* as the United States of America.

Civil government in the United States did not originate in a deliberate attempt to establish it; it was the outgrowth of the incorporation of profit-seeking ventures chartered by the Crown to operate upon American soil. The first of such being the incorporation of the London Virginia Company and its settlement in Jamestown, Virginia, in 1607, and then the Massachusetts Bay Colony and its settlement in America in 1630 are illustrations of this procedure. These charters and subsequent colonizations invested in the colonizing incorporations the essential characteristics of self-governing states. Ultimately, the commercial charters atrophied, leaving the residuum of civil government.

The 1770's saw the breakdown of British authority within the several colonies and the creation of individual state constitutions, embodying with modifications a readoption in constitutional form of their former charters.

These revolutionary state constitutions authorized their legislators to exercise the sovereign powers that they had in fact already assumed, each state claiming the independent status of an independent nation.[23]

So acute was the feeling in the American colonies against British authority that there were self-appointed local groups of patriots first organized to agitate against British policies. These local groups later organized in towns or townships and then collectively organized as county circular committees. The county circular committees thereafter chose state committees; and the Continental Congress was the national convention of these organized partisan groups, although the First Continental Congress was called at the suggestion of several of the provincial state congresses.

It is to be noted that in no sense had the Congress convened for the purpose of governing. During the first five weeks, it merely passed resolutions consisting of recommendations to the states *for their approval*. While it thereafter exercised certain powers in relation to the thirteen states, it at no time acted on delegated authority and was but a "diplomatic assembly" and did little more than unify the efforts of the states by providing special committees for common action.[24]

There was a total lack of special authority or any authority from the thirteen states or from any of them for or to the Continental Congress to act in any capacity whatsoever.

One of the first actions of the Continental Congress was the adoption of the Declaration of Rights, on October 14, 1774. In this respect it is to be noted that the Declaration of Rights speaks severally of the colonies as "The good people of the several Colonies. . . have severally. . . constituted. . . deputies. . . to. . . sit. . . in a full and free representation *of these Colonies.* . . ."[25] (Italics by author.) Also in said Declaration in resolution number 5, the Congress declared, "That the respective Colonies are entitled. . . ."[26]

May, 1775, was set for the meeting of the Second Continental Congress.

But in April, 1775, armed rebellion had commenced against British troops and British authority and the Battles of Lexington and Concord had been fought, armed clashes had occurred in Virginia, and the major battle of Bunker Hill was in the offing.

In August of 1775, the King proclaimed rebellion in the states, blockade of all colonial ports, and military engagements for the suppression of the rebellion. It is to be noted at this time that the War of the Revlolution was on. From the colonial standpoint severance of all English authority and rights had terminated. At this time the only constitutional authority, external or internal, in America was the independent and several American colonies or states acting as independent units, seeking their independence.

Events moved rapidly toward the establishment of formal independence in the early months of 1776. On May 10, the Continental Congress *called upon the thirteen colonies to create regular state governments.* On May 15, in a preamble to the resolution, it stated that, since Great Britain was making war upon the several colonies, all governmental authority under the Crown should be totally suppressed *and all governmental powers transferred to the people of the several colonies.*[27]

On June 7, Richard Henry Lee, acting on instructions from the State of Virginia, proposed to the Continental Congress the adoption of the following resolution: *"Resolved, that these united Colonies are, and of right ought to be, free and independent States, that they are absolved from all allegiance to the British Crown, and that all political connection between them and the State of Great Britain is, and ought to be totally dissolved. . . ."*[28] (Italics by author.) The foregoing resolution was referred to a committee of five members of the Congress and the result was the ultimate adoption on July 4, 1776, of the Declaration of Independence.[29] The Declaration was mostly the work of Thomas Jefferson, although Adams and Franklin suggested minor alterations. Actually, the salient features were borrowed almost verbatim from the philosophy and the theory of governement as expressed by John Locke in his Second Treatise.[30]

Analyzed carefully, the Declaration again shows the complete intention of the people of the thirteen colonies to institute at that time a government of free and independent states, not bound by any common unit nor by any common sovereign or government in any capacity whatsoever.

The Declaration contains four political ideas:

1. The doctrine of natural law and natural rights.
2. The compact theory of the state.
3. The doctrine of popular sovereignty.
4. The right of revolution.[31]

The principle of natural law and the sovereignty of the individual in the creation of government and the principle that the government and the state are to be maintained for the benefit of the individual and that sovereignty flows from the people are to be found in this Declaration. "We hold these truths to be self-evident, that all men are created equal, that they are endowed by their Creator with certain inalienable Rights, that among these are Life, Liberty, and the pursuit of Happiness. *That to secure these rights, Governments are instituted among Men, deriving their just powers from the consent of the governed.* That whenever any Form of Government becomes destructive of these ends, it is the Right of the People to alter or to abolish it, and to institute new Government. . . ."[32] (Italics by author.)

It may therefore be stated that the Declaration of Independence consummated the Revolution that found its inception in the Battles of Lexington and Concord in the early months of 1775. From the standpoint of the Constitution, the Revolution and the Revolutionary War must not be confused.

The Revolution, consummated by the Declaration of Independence, transferred all power and sovereignty from Great Britain to the States or colonies. The War of the Revolution was fought to confirm this transfer of power.

The political and sovereign entity of the thirteen colonies therefore were maintained in this status from the inception of the Revolutionary War until January 30, 1781, when the Articles of Confederation were finally ratified by the State of Maryland. It may well be noted at this point that, because of the complete severance of all sovereign powers by the thirteen original states or colonies, the Articles of Confederation required the complete consent of all thirteen states before becoming effective in any wise. It follows that, for a period of at least seven years, all thirteen states operated and existed individually and severally, externally as well as internally, as individual and separate nation or countries.

This brief but factual chronological history of the events immediately preceding and succeeding the War of the Revolution clearly shows that, contrary to the assertions of Justice Sutherland, all powers of external sovereignty passed from the Crown to the several colonies as separate and independent states and that the colonies were not a unit in foreign affairs nor acting through any delegated or lawful agency until the ratification of the Articles of Confederation on January 30, 1781. When the external sovereignty of Great Britain ceased, it was assumed in all respects by the colonies or the people thereof.

The treaty of peace referred to in the Curtiss-Wright opinion, executed September 3, 1783, was concluded between Great Britain and the United States of America, inasmuch as at that time the colonies were operating in respect to negotiating with foreign countries as a then unit under the Articles of Confederation.[33]

Contrary to Justice Sutherland's statement in the same case, the thirteen original states did possess all peculiar features of sovereignty. The statement that they could not make war is belied by the very fact that they did make war as individual states and that they successfully concluded the same war in the War of the Revolution. The statement that they could not make alliances or treaties is incorrect, at least up to the execution of the Articles of Confederation in January 1781. The fact that there was no opportunity or that the situation was not presented to any of the thirteen original states by which they were called upon to make a treaty or alliance does not prove nor can the conclusions be drawn therefrom that the right did not exist.

The Constitution Refutes Sutherland

The subsequent conclusions of Justice Sutherland that all the external powers of the United States are powers vested in the United States as concomitants of nationality, even if they had never been mentioned in the Federal Constitution, are conclusions that do not find their sanction in American constitutional government. They set up as a standard for their righteousness the powers exercised by other nations. They overlook entirely the Tenth Amendment to the Constitution and the express mandates of the Constitution that the Federal Government exists only on a grant of powers. If the contentions that the powers of the President include the power to make executive agreements that are not limited by constitutional powers or laws made pursuant thereto were correct, it follows that the legislative powers of the Congress are subordinate to any executive agreement made by the President, that under such power the President of the United States may enact by contract with foreign governments any law under the color of an executive agreement, and that such agreement becomes the law of the land.[34] *This constitutes a government of decree and not of law.* It is no longer a government under the Constitution but is a government under the Executive power.

The conclusion in the opinion that the powers of the Federal government did not exist upon affirmative grants of the Constitution belies and denies the very essence of the organic act itself and denies its all-embracing principle that all sovereignty flows from the people and that the government derives its powers from the governed. It is a conclusion that is made and would have to be made, by entirely overlooking the Constitution and its grant of powers.

Conclusion

The contention that the President is the sole organ of the nation in its external relations and its sole representative with foreign nations is not denied; the contention that he manages our concerns with foreign nations and must necessarily be most competent to determine when, how, and upon what subjects negotiations may be urged with the greatest prospect of success is not denied; and the conclusion that upon this vast external realm – with its important, complicated, delegate, and manifold problems – the President alone has the power to speak or listen as a representative of the nation is properly urged. *But this is the extent of the President's authority under the Constitution* and this is as far as he can legally or constitutionally go. From that point on if he negotiates a treaty, the treaty must be subject to the approval of two-thirds of the United States Senate present. If he concludes an executive agreement and does not present the same to the United States Senate as a treaty for its consent but chooses to ignore the United States Senate and term the same an agreement or compact, he acts unlawfully. The powers assumed are extraconstitutional and do not flow from the Constitution nor can they be found within the Constitution or as properly incidental to any of the powers of the President.

Such self-assumed powers create a government of unlimited power, because it is subject to no restraint whatsoever. Such powers constitute a government by decree or fiat for the same reason. All such unlawful assumptions of power and constitutional disregards are to be found not in the Constitution but in the practice of other nations or in the effectiveness of the immediate action. Such demands and assumptions of power by the Executive Department of the Federal Government are not only demands but are seizures of unlimited rights of government under the pretense of the conduct of foreign affairs through executive agreements. It is the seizure of unlimited power under this pretense.

The people of this country are asked to relinquish such unlimited powers to the Executive Department, actually to the President of the United States. The price paid for such relinquishment by the people and the assumption of such powers by the President would be and are all of the rights acquired through the War of the Revolution and the rights set up and guaranteed under the Constitution; and these are the sovereign rights of the People to govern themselves, to prescribe their own laws, and to delegate their own officers and agents to consummate the laws and to enforce the laws that they themselves have made.

Notes

[1]This essay originally appeared in the *Baylor Law Review*, VI (Spring, 1954), 277.

[2]Roscoe Pound, as quoted in C. Perry Patterson's *Presidential Government in the United States: The Unwritten Constitution* (Chapel Hill: The University of North Carolina Press, 1947), p. 143.

[3]"Executive agreements" may be chiefly illustrated as protocols, cartels, modi vivendi, and postal conventions. They may also be described as executive agreements entered into by the President as Commander-in-Chief of the Armed Forces of the United States. Two notable examples are the "Protocol of Agreement embodying the Terms of a Basis for the Establishment of Peace between *Spain* and the *United States*," signed at Washington on August 12, 1898 (Clive Parry [ed. and annot.], *The Consolidated Treaty Series* [Dobbs Ferry, New York: Oceana Publications, Inc., 1979], CLXXXVI, 408), and "Final Protocol between *Austria-Hungary, Belgium, France, Germany, Great Britain, Italy, Japan*, the *Netherlands, Russia, Spain* and the *United States* and *China* for the Resumption of Friendly Relations," signed at Peking on September 7, 1901 (*ibid.*, CXC, 61).

The writer feels that any exercise of such power must be strictly in conformity with the principles set forth in this article.

[4]*Asakura* v. *City of Seattle*, 265 U.S. 332, 68 L. Ed. 1041, 44 S. Ct. 515 (1924); *Valentine* v. *United States*,

299 U.S. 5, 81 L. Ed. 5, 299 S. Ct. 100 (1936); *United States v. Pink*, 315 U.S. 203, 86 L. Ed. 796, 62 S. Ct. 552 (1942).

[5]Article II, Sec. 2, Clause 2, U.S. Constitution.

[6]*Block v. Hirsh*, 256 U.S. 135, 65 L. Ed. 865, 41 S. Ct. 458 (1921); *Ashwander v. The Tennessee Valley Authority*, 297 U.S. 288, 80 L. Ed. 688, 56 S. Ct. 466 (1936); *United States v. Darby*, 312 U.S. 100, 85 L. Ed. 609, 61 S. Ct. 451 (1941); *Wickard v. Filburn*, 317 U.S. 111, 87 L. Ed. 122, 63 S. Ct. 82 (1942); *Mulford v. Smith*, 307 U.S. 38, 83 L. Ed. 1092, 59 S. Ct. 648 (1939); *Hamilton v. Kentucky Distilleries & Warehouse Co.*, 251 U.S. 146, 64 L. Ed. 194, 40 S. Ct. 106 (1919); *Woods v. Cloyd W. Miller Co.*, 333 U.S. 144, 92 L. Ed. 602, 68 S. Ct. 424 (1948); *Bowles v. Willingham*, 321 U.S. 503, 88 L. Ed. 892, 64 S. Ct. 641 (1944); *Yakus v. United States*, 321 U.S. 414, 88 L. Ed. 834, 64 S. Ct. 660 (1944); *Norman v. Baltimore & Ohio Railroad Co.* and *United States v. Bankers Trust Co.* (the Gold Clause Cases), 294 U.S. 240, 79 L. Ed. 885, 55 S. Ct. 407 (1935); and Joseph L. Call, "The Drift from the Constitution," U.S. Congress, House, *Congressional Record*, 82nd Cong., 1st sess., 1951, 97, pt. 1: 1166; and *op. cit.*, *Los Angeles Bar Bulletin*, XXVI (January, 1951), 163. [In the above essay, the author discusses nearly all of the above cases and other cases, *inter alia*.]

[7]*Kansas v. Colorado*, 206 U.S. 89-90, 51 L. Ed. 971, 27 S. Ct. 664 (1907), the Preamble to the Constitution, and the Declaration of Independence of July 4, 1776.

[8]Amendment X, United States Constitution.

[9]Benjamin Franklin, as quoted in *The Records of the Federal Convention of 1787*, ed. by Max Farrand (rev. ed.;

New Haven and London: Yale University Press, 1966) I, 102-103.

[10]Edward S. Corwin, *The President: Office and Powers* (4th ed. rev.; New York: New York University Press, 1957), p. 177.

[11]Wilfred E. Binkley and Malcolm C. Moos, *A Grammar of American Politics: The National Government* (3rd ed. rev.; New York: Alfred A. Knoph, Inc., 1958, pp. 316-317.

[12]"Collection and Disbursement of Customs Revenues" is such an executive agreement. (Clive Parry [ed. and annotator], *The Consolidated Treaty Series* [Dobbs Ferry, New York: Oceana Publications, Inc., 1980], CXCVIII, p. 208.)

[13]The American Bar Association has purposed the following Constitutional Amendment:

> Executive agreements shall not be made in lieu of treaties. Congress shall have power to enforce this provision by appropriate legislation. Nothing herein shall be construed to restrict the existing power of Congress to regulate executive agreements under the provisions of the Constitution. ["Report of the Standing Committee on Peace and Law through United Nations," *Annual Report of the American Bar Association* (Baltimore: the Lord Baltimore Press, 1952), LXXVII, 244.]

[14]Charles Warren, *The Supreme Court in United States History* (Boston and Toronto: Little, Brown, and Co., 1926), pp. 748-749.

[15]Patterson, *op. cit.*, pp. 12-13.

[16]Ernest Sutherland Bates, *The Story of the*

Supreme Court (Indianapolis: Bobbs-Merrill Co., 1936; and Littleton, Colorado: Fred B. Rothman & Co., 1982), p. 42. (© 1936 Bobbs-Merrill Co.)

[17]Farrand, *op. cit.*, II, 163 *et. seq.*; "The Compact Clause of the Constitution – A Study in Interstate Adjustments," Felix Frankfurter and James M. Landis, *Yale Law Journal*, XXXIV (May, 1925), 685; and "Executive Agreements: a Study of the Executive in the Control of the Foreign Relations of the United States," David M. Levitan, *Illinois Law Review*, XXXV (December, 1940), 365.

[18]*Downes* v. *Bidwell*, 182 U.S. 312, 45 L. Ed. 1116, 21 S. Ct. 797 (1901).

[19]George Sutherland, *Constitutional Power and World Affairs* (New York: Columbia University Press, 1919; and Johnson Reprint Corporation., 1970).

[20]*Ibid.*, pp. 170-172; and Charles Henry Butler, *The Treaty-Making Power of the United States* (New York: The Banks Law Publishing Co., 1902), I, 5.

[21]Sutherland, *op. cit.*, p. 171. **JLC**.

Justice Sutherland's lack of respect for the fact that our government under the Constitution is one of enumerated powers is indicated by the following:

> We must cease to measure the authority of the general government only by what the Constitution affirmatively grants, and consider it also in the light of what the Constitution permits from failure to deny. [*Ibid.*, p. 172.]

By applying this stunning doctrine to treaty-making powers of the government as Sutherland would (and as he and others have applied it), we clearly have a dangerously arrogant misapplication of, perversion of, and extension of the Tenth Amendment to the Federal Government itself. **JEN.**

[22]*United States* v. *Curtiss-Wright Corporation*, (299 U.S. 304, 81 L. Ed. 255, 57 S. Ct. 216 (1936).

[23]Binkley and Moos, *op. cit.*, p. 24.

[24]C. H. Van Tyne, "Continental Congress," *Cyclopedia of American Government*, eds. Andrew C. McLaughlin and Albert Bushnell, Vol. I (1963).

[25]Henry Steel Commager (ed.), *Documents of American History* (9th ed.; Englewood Clffis, New Jersey: Prentice-Hall, Inc., 1973), I, 83.

[26]*Ibid.*

[27]Alfred H. Kelly and Winfred A. Harbison, *The American Constitution: Its Origins and Development* (rev. ed.; New York: W. W. Norton & Co., Inc., 1955), p. 88.

[28]Commager, *op. cit.*, p. 100.

[29]*Ibid.*

[30]John Locke, "An Essay Concerning the True Original Extent and End of Civil Government," *Two Treatises of Government* (London: J. M. Dent & Sons Ltd., 1924), pp. 117-242.

[31]Kelly and Harbison, *op. cit.*, p. 90.

[32]Commager, *op. cit.*, p. 100.

[33]"Definitive Treaty of Peace between the United States of America and His Britannic Majesty," 8 Stat. 80.

[34]"The argument," wrote Henry Adams in *The Life of Albert Gallatin*, was "irrestible; it was never answered; and indeed the mere statement is enough to leave only a sense of surprise that the Federalists should have hazarded themselves on such preposterous ground." (Henry Adams, *The Life of Albert Gallatin* [New York: Peter Smith, 1943], p. 161.)

Appendices

Appendix I

Ideological War

James Ervin Norwood

The communists are using essentially the same method to conquer the United States and indeed the world that they used to conquer Czechoslovakia. Their final act in that country was preceded by more than a generation of infiltration of Marxian premises into the thinking of the people. This intellectual process was the real conquest, while the coup d'etat that made headlines in 1948 was only the icing on the communist cake.

In the decades preceding their seizing of power, they left the form of the law or the outer shell to maintain an illusion that nothing had changed, while they gradually and cumulatively grossly removed the content or changed the meaning of the law and replaced it with revolutionary content or meaning.

They infiltrated the media, the publishing houses, the courts, legislatures, executive branches, armed forces, police, bureaucracies, schools and universities, seminaries, churches and synagogues, and professional associations, first with ideas and then with sympathizers, fellow-travelers, and communists.

Having surrounded Czechoslovakia with an overwhelming and intimidating Red Army after World War II, they organized armed terrorist bands to disarm the people and enforce land reform laws that had been drafted not from guns but from ideas.

You can get the Czechoslovak plan directly from the horse's mouth in Jan Kozak's *And Not a Shot is Fired*.[1]

We are well along the way toward a Czechoslovak-type takeover, after some two generations of infiltration and subversion of our judiciary. It was hardly an accident that Alger Hiss, who was imprisoned for perjury in denying that he was a member of the Communist Party, was a law clerk for Justice Felix Frankfurter of the United States Supreme Court. How many more law clerks and even judges with similar persuasions have we had in our judicial system over the years, and how many of them are in the courts right now? How much influence did Hiss have with Frankfurter, and how much influence did Frankfurter have with the other Justices of the Supreme Court? It is fair to ask how much influence Hiss had with the Justices of the Supreme Court, since two of them testified as character witnesses at his trial. How often was Hiss instrumental in getting the critical vote or votes in five-four decisions? How much has our Constitution been rewritten in red ink by the communists, with such agents as Hiss?

How much has our Constitution been perverted, by the infiltration of Marxian premises into the minds of law clerks and judges via textbooks in the social sciences? One can get a clue, by checking the premises in the theoretical works of the communists and then reading the strange decisions emerging from our leftist Supreme Court from the 1930's to date and therein finding many of the same premises. Such distortions of the Constitution that one can find in *Berman v. Parker*, 348 U.S. 26, 99 L. Ed. 27, 75 S. Ct. 98 (1954); in *U.S. v. Enmons*, 410 U.S. 396, 35 L. Ed. 2nd 379, 93 S. Ct. 1007 (1973); and in *Hawaii Housing Authority v. Midkiff*, 467 U.S. 229, 81 L. Ed. 2nd 186, 104 S. Ct. 2321 (1984), can be traced not to the Constitution or its Signers but to some of the doctrines preached by Karl Marx, Frederick Engels, Vladimir Lenin, Joseph Stalin, Nicolai Bukharin, and Mao Tse-tung. One might compare many of the premises in our textbooks in the social sciences with the premises in the writings of Marx, Engels, Lenin, Stalin, Bukharin, and Mao to pick up the strands of the Red rope that has been used to lynch the Constitution (and that has been used to found legislation, public policies, and foreign policies). The perversion of the General Welfare Clause alone into a wild card, largely through Marxian ideological influence, has devastated and gutted the Constitution, very nearly voided it with respect to property rights and thus human rights, and made a shambles of Federalism.

One can examine the writings of the communists to recognize their use in the formation of public opinion through the minds of the thought leaders. The evidence is massive and tangible that we have been had by the most subtle and effective kind of conquest in human history: conquest of the mind. In military parlance, you could call their method of conquest ideological envelopment.[2]

A logical response or remedy is an ideological counterthrust. It is my opinion that we can not only counter it successfully but have superior ideologies with which to intellectually undermine and wipe out their illogical ideology.[3]

As soon as we get our ideologies on the battlefield, we will start winning this fist fight.[4]

85

Notes

[1]Jan Kozak, *And Not a Shot Is Fired: The Communist Strategy for Subverting a Representative Government* (Wilton, Connecticut: The Long House, 1972).

The author was a member of the Secretariat of the Communist Party of Czechoslovakia.

The author's title of the work is *How Parliament Can Play a Revolutionary Part in the Transition to Socialism, and the Role of the Popular Masses.*

As you read through this 48-page handbook, you will see striking similarities between the application of its principles in the takeover of Czechoslovakia and their application in the takeover of the United States.

[2]The United States Government and the U.S.S.R. are now putting into action a plan to Sovietize American elementary and secondary schools. The plan proceeds from an agreement between the U.S. and the Soviets that was signed on November 21, 1985, at Geneva. The title of the agreement is "The General Agreement between the Government of the United States of America and the Government of the Union of Soviet Socialist Republics on Contacts, Exchanges and Coöperation in Scientific, Technical, Educational, Cultural and other Fields." The plan is now in the beachhead stage and that is the point at which to knock it out, since it is a one-way street for Soviet indoctrination of our children.

Private foundations that are tax exempt are to handle details of the plan that would be unseemly, illegal, and unconstitutional for the U.S. Government to handle. Indeed, a private foundation negotiated the plan with the Soviets, at the request of the U.S. Department of State.

(*Phyllis Schlafly Report*, XXI [September, 1987], Section 2.)

A self-addressed stamped envelope with your request for the article, entitled "Will We Let the Soviets Teach Our Schoolchildren?" will get you the sordid details. Your SASE and request should be sent to the *Phyllis Schlafly Report*, P.O. Box 618, Alton, Illinois 62002, 1-618-462-5415.

[3]The main reason that the communists have been winning is that, from their delusional ideology, they have derived a will to win, while the West has abandoned its ideology from which it could have developed a will to win and bought Marxism. From that it has literally developed a will to lose and accomodate its ideological allies in the East.

The Western response to communism from 1917 to date has been a mixture of half-hearted opposition to communism and a sometimes whole-hearted financing of communism. While the right hand has jabbed in defense to make retreat tenable, the left hand has shook hands in surrender to and support of communism. This clumsy and suicidal schizophrenia has its roots in the communist-directed suppression of our ideology of free capitalistic enterprise and equality before the law and our communist-promoted adoption of the Marxian ideology.

[4]The battlefield is the realm of human thought.

Appendix II

Writings That One Can Read and Study to Regenerate the Law of the Constitution and Capitalism

James Ervin Norwood

By reading and studying some theoretical works of capitalism and related diagnostic works and writings on constitutional law, classical liberal political science, history, sociology, psychology, philosophy, and education that are cited below, you can refute the prevailing ideologies of Marxism, Marxism-Leninism, Keynesianism, monetarism and the rest of the trash in the statist junkyard that hve been used by the mistaken to subvert the Constitution; and you can simultaneously adopt, with your reading of the same books, a positive alternative in the ideology of free capitalistic enterprise and equality before the law. The results will be the rebirth of the Constitution and ultimately the induction of a global free market from soul to soul and from Pole to Pole, which will generate world peace and general prosperity.

The Bibliography

(1) Ludwig von Mises, *Economic Policy: Thoughts for Today and Tomorrow* (South Bend, Indiana: Regnery Gateway, 1979).

(2) Ludwig von Mises, *Liberalism: A Socio-Economic Exposition*, trans. Ralph Raico and Arthur Goddard (Kansas City: Sheed Andrews and McMeel, Inc., 1978).

(3) Ludwig von Mises, *Bureaucracy* (New Rochelle, New York: Arlington House, 1969).

(4) Ludwig von Mises, *The Anti-Capitalistic Mentality* (South Holland, Illinois: Libertarian Press, 1972).

(5) Murray N. Rothbard, "Economic Depressions: Their Cause and Cure," *The Austrian Theory of the Trade Cycle and Other Essays* (New York: Center for Libertarian Studies, 1978), p. 21.

(6) Murray N. Rothbard, *What Has Government Done to Our Money?* (Santa Ana, California: Rampart College Publications, 1974).

(7) Hans F. Sennholz, *Gold Is Money* (Westport, Connecticut: Greenwood Press, 1975).

(8) Percy L. Greaves, Jr. *Is Further Intervention a Cure for Prior Intervention?* Irvington-on-Hudson, New York: The Foundation for Economic Education, 1956).

(9) Garet Garrett, *The People's Pottage (Caldwell, Idaho: The Caxton Printers, Ltd., 1965).*

(10) Karl Brandt and others, *The Farm Problem* (Irvington-on-Hudson, New York: The Foundation for Economic Education, 1986.)

(11) Clarence B. Carson, *Throttling the Railroads* (Irvington-on-Hudson, New York: The Foundation for Economic Education, 1971.)

(12) Henry Hazlitt, *The Inflation Crisis and How to Resolve It* (New Rochelle, New York: Arlington House, 1978).

(13) Joan Kennedy Taylor (ed.) *Free Trade: The Necessary Foundation for World Peace* (Irvington-on-Hudson, New York: The Foundation for Economic Education, 1986).

(14) Hans F. Sennholz, *Age of Inflation* (Belmont, Massachusetts: Western Islands, 1979).

(15) W. M. Curtiss, *The Tariff Idea* (Irvington-on-Hudson, New York: The Foundation for Economic Education, 1953).

(16) Henry Hazlitt, *Economics in One Lesson* (New Rochelle, New York: Arlington House, 1979).

(17) Percy L. Greaves, Jr. *Mises Made Easier* (Dobbs Ferry, New York: Free Market Books, 1974).

(18) Gustavo R. Velasco, *Labor Legislation from an Economic Point of View,* ed. Benjamin A. Rogge (Indianapolis: Liberty Fund, 1973).

(19) Faustino Ballvé, *Essentials of Economics*, trans. and ed. Arthur Goddard (Irvington-on-Hudson, New York: The Foundation for Economic Education, 1963).

(20) Bettina Bien Greaves (ed.), *Free Market Economics: A Basic Reader* (Irvington-on-Hudson, New York: The Foundation for Economic Education, 1975).

(21) Murray N. Rothbard, *The Case for a 100 Percent Gold Dollar* (Washington: Libertarian Review Press, 1974).

(22) Murray N. Rothbard, *Education, Free and Compulsory: The Individual's Education* (Wichita, Kansas: Center for Independent Education, 1972).

(23) Andrew Dickson White, *Fiat Money Inflation in*

France (Irvington-on-Hudson, New York: The Foundation for Economic Education, 1959).

(24) Hans F. Sennholz, *Death and Taxes* (2nd ed. rev.; Cedar Falls, Iowa: Center for Futures Education, 1982).

(25) Ludwig von Mises, *On Current Monetary Problems*, interv. Percy L. Greaves, Jr. (Lansing, Michigan: Constitutional Alliance, 1969).

(26) Howard S. Katz, *The Paper Aristocracy* (New York: Books In Focus, Inc., 1976).

(27) Ludwig von Mises, *Planning for Freedom* (South Holland, Illinois: Libertarian Press, 1980).

(28) F. A. Harper, *An Introduction to Value Theory* (Menlo Park, California: Institute for Humane Studies, 1974).

(29) Percy L. Greaves, Jr. *Understanding the Dollar Crisis* (Belmont, Massachusetts: Western Islands, 1973).

(30) Murray N. Rothbard, *For a New Liberty: The Libertarian Manifesto* (rev. ed.; New York: Collier Books; and London: Collier MacMillan Publishers, 1978).

(31) "Selections from *Human Action*," ed. George Koether, *The Freeman* (September, 1981), 518-572.

(32) Ludwig von Mises, *The Historical Setting of the Austrian School of Economics* (New Rochelle, New York: Arlington House, 1969).

(33) Ludwig von Mises, *Socialism: An Economic and Sociological Analysis*, trans. J. Kahane (Indianapolis: Liberty Fund, 1981).

(34) Bettina Bien Greaves, *Free Market Economics: A Syllabus* (Irvington-on-Hudson, New York: The Foundation for Economic Education, 1975).

(35) Ludwig von Mises, *Nation, State, and Economy: Contributions to the Politics and History of Our Time*, trans.

Leland B. Yeager (New York and London: New York University Press, 1983).

(36) Murray N. Rothbard, *Power and Market: Government and the Economy* (Kansas City: Sheed Andrews and McMeel, Inc. 1977).

(37) Israel M. Kirzner, *Market Theory and the Price System* (New York: D. Van Nostrand, Co., 1963).

(38) Murray N. Rothbard, *America's Great Depression* (Kansas City: Sheed and Ward, Inc., 1975).

(39) Murray N. Rothbard, *Man, Economy, and State: A Treatise on Economic Principles* (Kansas City: Sheed Andrews and McMeel, Inc. 1978).

(40) Israel M. Kirzner, *Competition and Entrepreneurship* (Chicago: University of Chicago Press, 1973).

(41) Israel M. Kirzner, *Perception, Opportunity, and Profit: Studies in the Theory of Entrepreneurship* (Chicago: University of Chicago Press, 1979).

(42) Israel M. Kirzner, *The Economic Point of View: An Essay in the History of Economic Thought* (Kansas City: Sheed and Ward, Inc., 1976).

(43) Ludwig von Mises, *Notes and Recollections*, trans. Hans F. Sennholz (South Holland, Illinois: Libertarian Press, 1978).

(44) Ludwig von Mises, *A Critique of Interventionism: Inquiries into the Economic Policy and the Economic Ideology of the Present*, trans. Hans F. Sennholz (New Rochelle, New York: Arlington House, 1977).

(45) Ludwig von Mises, *On the Manipulation of Money and Credit*, trans. Bettina Bien Greaves, ed. Percy L. Greaves, Jr. (Dobbs Ferry, New York: Free Market Books. 1978).

(46) Ludwig von Mises, *The Theory of Money and*

Credit, trans. H. E. Batson (Irvington-on-Hudson, New York: The Foundation for Economic Education, 1971).

(47) Ludwig von Mises, *Omnipotent Government: The Rise of the Total State and Total War* (New Rochelle, New York: Arlington House, 1969).

(48) Ludwig von Mises, *Theory and History: An Interpretation of Social and Economic Evolution* (New Rochelle, New York: Arlington House, 1969).

(49) Ludwig von Mises, *The Ultimate Foundations of Economic Science: An Essay on Method* (Kansas City: Sheed Andrews and McMeel, Inc., 1978).

(50) Ludwig von Mises, *Epistemological Problems of Economics*, trans. George Reisman (New York and London: New York University Press, 1981).

(51) Israel M. Kirzner, *Discovery and the Capitalist Process* (Chicago: University of Chicago Press, 1985).

(52) T. S. Ashton and others, *Capitalism and the Historians*, ed. F. A. Hayek (Chicago: University of Chicago Press, 1954).

(53) Ludwig von Mises, *Human Action: A Treatise on Economics* (Chicago: Henry Regnery Co., 1966).

(54) W. H. Hutt, *Keynesianism – Retrospect and Prospect* (Chicago: Henry Regnery Co., 1963).

(55) Leonard E. Read, *Instead of Violence* (Lansing, Michigan: Bramble Minibooks, 1973).

(56) W. H. Hutt, *The Economics of the Colour Bar* (London: Institute of Economic Affairs, 1964).

(57) Leonard E. Read and others, *Clichés of Socialism* (Irvington-on-Hudson, New York: The Foundation for Economic Education, 1970).

(58) W. H. Hutt, *The Theory of Collective Bargaining, 1930-1975* (London: The Institute of Economic Af-

fairs, 1975).

(59) Sylvester Petro, "Sovereignty and Compulsory Public-Sector Bargaining," *Wake Forest Law Review*, X (March, 1974), 25.

(60) W. H. Hutt, *The Theory of Idle Resources: A Study in Definition* (Indianapolis: Liberty Fund, 1977).

(61) Frank A. Fetter, *Capital, Interest, and Rent: Essays in the Theory of Distribution*, ed. Murray N. Rothbard (Kansas City: Sheed Andrews and McMeel, Inc., 1977).

(62) *Individual Freedom: Selected Works of William H. Hutt*, eds. Svetozar Pejovich and David Klingman (Westport, Connecticut, and London: Greenwood Press, 1975).

(63) Sven Rydenfelt, *A Pattern for Failure: Socialist Economies in Crisis* (San Diego, New York, and London: Harcourt Brace Jovanovich, Publishers, 1984).

(64) W. H. Hutt, *The Keynesian Episode: A Reassessment* (Indianapolis: Liberty Fund, 1979).

(65) Murray N. Rothbard, *The Ethics of Liberty* (Atlantic Highlands, New Jersey: Humanities Press, 1982).

(66) W. H. Hutt, *A Rehabilitation of Say's Law* (Athens: Ohio University Press, 1975).

(67) W. H. Hutt, *The Strike-Threat System: The Economic Consequences of Collective Bargaining* (New Rochelle, New York: Arlington House, 1973).

(68) Ayn Rand, *Capitalism: The Unknown Ideal* (New York: The New American Library, Inc., 1966).

(69) Elgin Groseclose, *America's Money Machine: The Story of the Federal Reserve* (Westport, Connecticut: Arlington House, 1980).

(70) John Hospers and others, *The Libertarian Alter-

native, ed. Tibor R. Machan (Chicago: Nelson-Hall Co., 1974).

(71) Elgin Groseclose, *Money and Man: A Survey of Monetary Experience* (4th ed. rev.; Norman: University of Oklahoma Press, 1976).

(72) Adam Smith and others, *The Capitalist Reader*, ed. Lawrence S. Stepelevich (New Rochelle, New York: Arlington House, 1977).

(73) Bruno Leoni, *Freedom and the Law* (Los Angeles: Nash Publishing, 1972).

(74) Bernard H. Siegan, *Land Use without Zoning* (Lexington, Massachusetts; Toronto; and London: D. C. Heath and Co., 1972).

(75) James Rolph Edwards, *The Economist of the Country: Ludwig von Mises in the History of Monetary Thought* (New York: Carlton Press, Inc., 1985).

(76) Frederic Bastiat, *The Law*, trans. Dean Russell (Irvington-on-Hudson, New York: The Foundation for Economic Education, 1950).

(77) Sylvestor Petro, "Separation of Powers and the Labor Act: I. Congressional Policies versus Labor Board Policies," the *Freeman*, XVIII (July, 1968), 402-414; "II. 'Expertise,' Separation of Powers, and Due Process" (August, 1968), 497-506; "III. Judicial Courts versus Administrative Courts" (September, 1968), 553-566.

(78) Sylvestor Petro, "Compulsory Public-Sector Bargaining," the *Freeman*, XXV (August, 1975), 494-508.

(79) Sylvestor Petro, "Unemployment, Unions and Inflation: of Causation and Necessity," the *Freeman*, XXVI (July, 1976), 387-403.

(80) D. T. Armentano, *The Myths of Antitrust: Economic Theory and Legal Cases* (New Rochelle, New

York: Arlington House, 1972).

(81) D. T. Armentano, *Antitrust Policy: The Case for Repeal* (Washington: Cato Institute, 1986).

(82) F. A. Hayek and others, *Verdict on Rent Control* (London: The Institute of Economic Affairs, 1972).

(83) D. T. Armentano, *Antitrust and Monopoly: Anatomy of a Policy Failure* (New York: John Wiley & Son, Inc., 1982.)

(84) Lord Robbins, *Political Economy Past and Present: A Review of Leading Theories of Economic Policy* (New York: Columbia University Press, 1976).

(85) Gabriel Kolko, *Railroads and Regulation: 1877-1916* (New York and London: W. W. Norton & Co., 1965).

(86) Trygve J. B. Hoff, *Economic Calculation in the Socialist Society* (Indianapolis: Liberty Fund, 1981).

(87) Helmut Schoeck, *Envy: A Theory of Social Behaviour* (New York: Harcourt, Brace & World, Inc., 1969).

(88) Charles McKay, *Extraordinary Popular Delusions and the Madness of Crowds* (New York: Farrar, Straus and Giroux, Inc., 1932).

(89) Walter E. Williams, *The State Against Blacks* (New York, St. Louis, San Francisco, Hamburg, Mexico City, and Toronto: McGraw Hill Book Co., 1982).

(90) Brian Crozier and Arthur Seldon, *Socialism: The Grand Delusion* (New York: Universe Books, 1986).

(91) Thomas Sowell, *Race and Economics* (New York: David McKay Co., Inc., 1975).

(92) Robert L. Carneiro and others, *The Politicization of Society* (Indianapolis: Liberty Fund, 1979).

(93) Thomas Sowell, *Civil Rights: Rhetoric or Reali-*

ty? (New York: William Morrow and Co., Inc., 1984).

(94) Auberon Herbert, *The Right and Wrong of Compulsion by the State, and Other Essays* (Indianapolis: Liberty Fund, 1978).

(95) Thomas Sowell, *The Economics and Politics of Race: An International Perspective* (New York: William Morrow and Co., Inc., 1983).

(96) Gottfried Dietze, *In Defense of Property* (Baltimore and London: The Johns Hopkins Press, 1963.

(97) Henry Hazlitt, *Man vs. The Welfare State* (New Rochelle, New York: Arlington House, 1969).

(98) Gottfried Dietze, *America's Political Dilemma* (Baltimore: The Johns Hopkins Press, 1968).

(99) Thomas Sowell, *Marxism: Philosophy and Economics* (New York: William Morrow and Co., Inc., 1985).

(100) Henry Hazlitt, *The Conquest of Poverty* (New Rochelle, New York: Arlington House, 1973).

(101) Gottfried Dietze, *The Federalist: A Classic on Federalism and Free Government* (Baltimore: The Johns Hopkins Press, 1960).

(102) Bernard H. Siegan, *Economic Liberties and the Constitution* (Chicago: University of Chicago Press, 1981).

(103) Richard A. Epstein, *Takings: Private Property and the Power of Eminent Domain* (Cambridge: Harvard University Press, 1985).

(104) Henry Mark Holzer, *Sweet Land of Liberty? The Supreme Court and Individual Rights* (Corona Del Mar, California: Common Sense Press, 1983).

(105) Bernard H. Siegan, *The Supreme Court's Constitution: An Inquiry into Judicial Review and Its Impact on Society* (New Brunswick, New Jersey: Transaction

Books, 1986).

(106) *Money, Method, and the Market Process: Essays by Ludwig von Mises*, annot. Richard Ebeling (Auburn, Alabama: Ludwig von Mises Institute, 1988).

(107) *The Economics of Ludwig von Mises: An Annotated Bibliography*, ed. Richard Ebeling (Auburn, Alabama: Ludwig von Mises Institute, 1988).

(108) Hans F. Sennholz, *The Politics of Unemployment* (Spring Mills, Pennsylvania: Libertarian Press, 1987).

(109) Hans F. Sennholz, *Debts and Deficits* (Spring Mills, Pennsylvania: Libertarian Press, 1987).

Sources

Many of these books are in the inventory of the Ludwig von Mises Institute, Thatch Hall, Auburn University, Auburn, Alabama 36849, 1-205-826-2500. The Mises Institute gives books to students and teachers.

Even more of these books are in the inventory of the Foundation for Economic Education, 30 South Broadway, Irvington-on-Hudson, New York 10533, 1-914-591-7230. FEE has a program that loans books to students and teachers at no charge.

The above organizations are nonprofit and depend on tax-deductible contributions and revenue from sales.

Two commercial outlets that have most of these books are as follows:

Laissez Faire Books
522 Broadway, 7th Floor
New York, N.Y. 10012
1-800-238-2200, Ext. 500

Liberty Tree Network
6600 Silacci Way
Gilroy, Ca. 95020
1-800-345-2888

Progressivity

The bibliography is designed to be read in series to a point, as it moves from popular works that are relatively easy to read and understand to more difficult abstract works through about the first half of the entries. As soon as one is well founded and interested enough to break the sequence, he or she should move ahead to the big four, entries 33, 39, 46, and 53.

Popular Reading

With the popular reading, one can develop an interest in and working knowledge of the free market and a foundation for reading the abstract works.

The Abstract Works

By reading the abstract works, one can become a thought leader and can thus be a maker of history.

Interpretations and Applications

Just because a power is in the Constitution does not mean that it is wise to use that power to destroy freedom and prosperity or to use it at all. (Many such powers that can be abused should be nullified by amendment.) For example, all kinds of economic damage has been done by misapplications of the power to regulate interstate commerce, the power to tax, and the power to coin money. When the thought leaders and intellectuals in general seriously study the works in the bibliography, they can deal with the formation of public opinion against such destruction.

A lawyer or a judge who has not made a serious study of the works in the bibliography is not merely crippled intellectually. That person is both extremely dangerous and extremely negligent. A careful study of the above works is prerequisite to the responsible practice of law and to responsibly presiding over judicial proceedings.

When the books in the bibliography are read and discussed in the schools and when people in general read and discuss them, we will be well on the way to the end of war and an amazing prosperity.

We can and we must do the job in this century. If we neglect to do so, there might not be a next century for us. Whether we have a civilization or a few survivors in anarchy depends on what you do with the stuff between your ears in the next dozen years.

Recommended for Research

Articles that are associated with the books in the bibliography can be found in *The Freeman*, which is published by the Foundation for Economic Education; in *The Free Market* and the *Review of Austrian Economics*, which are published by the Ludwig von Mises Institute; and in *Econ* and *Econ Update*, which are published by the Reason Foundation (2716 Ocean Park Boulevard, Santa Monica, California 90405, 1-213-392-0443).

Most of these articles are popular reading. Many of them can be read without prerequisite reading in the bibliography, and are thus good starting points for developing a broader and deeper interest in free market reading. Most of them are very good for assignment to students. They are also good reading for the free market guerrilla, who might spin off letters to the editor that are based on them and in the process mention books that expand on them.

Ample leads for research can be found in *Murray N. Rothbard: A Scholar in Defense of Freedom*, comp. Carl Watner and annot. David Gordon (Auburn, Alabama: Ludwig von Mises Institute, 1986). This is Dr. Rothbard's bibliography and it is well worth working.

The Pacific Research Institute for Public Policy (177 Post Street, San Francisco, California 94108, 1-415-989-0833), the Cato Institute (224 Second Street S.E., Washington, D.C. 20003, 1-202-546-0200), and the Institute for Humane Studies (George Mason University, 4400 University Drive, Fairfax, Virginia 22030, 1-703-323-1055), have catalogues of books that are worth reading.

The Winners

When the History of World War III is written, it will be recorded that a Volunteer Army of Readers arose *en masse* to win it with the writings of a small cadre of diligent scholars.

Appendix III

The Relation between Property Rights and Human Liberty and Prosperity

James Ervin Norwood

Without respect for property rights to permit the accumulation of capital at least at the rate of growth in population, we can only fall back to the depths of poverty and disease, from which we arose with the protection of property rights.

Without property rights, there can be no human rights, for your property is the fruit of your labor. You are a slave to the extent that others seize your labor through the power of government to pursue their values, to impose their values on you, and to deprive you of the means to pursue some of your values.

The task to which we must address ourselves to save this civilization is the limitation of government power, in order to preserve property rights and thus human rights. This means the nullification of government power, except that power which is necessary to prevent people from infringing on each other's liberty or property and to prevent cruelty to animals. This means negations in constitutions that regulate government with law that is set in stone, not positive clauses through which people can go to seize the property of others and to interfere in commerce.

The result of protecting property rights will be an expansion of human liberty and the accumulation of capital at a faster rate than the growth in population. That will yield more private investment in tools and plant, in research, and in education per worker. Those increments will result in higher marginal productivity and higher wages, higher profits, and higher levels of living.

You can achieve respect for property rights and human liberty and prosperity, by reading and applying the works in the bibliography; and you can do it in this century.

We can advance our civilization only as far as we can advance our understanding of the relationship between property rights and liberty and apply what we have learned in our public policies and in our economic relationships.

Appendix IV

World War III

James Ervin Norwood

World War III has been raging wide open for more than forty years.

World War III is an ideological war. The weapons are ideas, not bombs. The battlefield is the human mind. The issue is private ownership of the means of production and thus their control by consumers under the principle of one penny-one vote versus state ownership of the means of production and their control by tyrants under the principle of one bullet-one ballot. The private system is directed ultimately by free consumers. The statist system is operated by the firing squad or punishment even unto death for dissenters to the state's commands.

If we lose World War III by default or otherwise to the mistaken statists, we will lose this civilization through the destruction of property rights and human liberty.

If we win World War III, we will rise to a higher civilization through the preservation of property rights and human liberty.

We can win World War III, by reading and applying the works in the bibliography and spreading the ideas in them at home and abroad.[1] Victory is the development of a global consensus for the protection of property rights and thus human rights via the limitation of government power.

Note

[1]Some additional readings that will help us win can be found in a number of great works of classical liberalism that are available from Liberty Fund, 7440 North Shadeland, Indianapolis, Indiana 46250, 1-317-842-0880. Although some of the economic theories in them are out-moded and should be revised by the works of Mises, they clearly put forth the bedrock principles, on which this civilization was founded. Without which principles free market economics would be impossible to apply and the Constitution itself would not only totally perish but would have never come into existence in the first place.

Obviously, we have some catching up to do, as we have been systematically cut off from our great heritage for decades by the Marxian monsters in the universities.

Appendix V

Human Rights
Are Property Rights[1]

Dr. Murray N. Rothbard[2]

Much is heard these days of the distinction between human rights and property rights; and many who claim to champion the one turn with scorn upon any defender of the other. They fail to see that property rights, far from being in conflict with human rights, are in fact the most basic of all human rights.

The human right of every person to his or her own life implies the right to find and transform resources: to *produce* that which sustains and advances life. That product is a person's property. That is why property rights are foremost among human rights and why any loss of one endangers the others. For example, how can the human right of freedom of the press be preserved, if the government owns all the newsprint and has the power to decide who may use it and how much? The human right of a free press depends on the human right to private property in newsprint and in other essentials for newspaper production.

In short, there is no conflict of rights between property rights and human rights, because property rights are themselves human rights. What is more, human rights are also property rights! There are several aspects of this important truth. In the first place, each individual, according to our understanding of the natural order of things, is the owner of himself or herself, the ruler of his or her own person. Preservation of this self-ownership is essential for the proper development and well-being of one's self. The human rights of the person are, in effect, a recognition of each person's inalienable property right over his or her own being; and from this property right stems that person's right to the material goods that he or she has produced. A person's right to personal freedom, then, is that person's property right in himself or herself.

But there is another sense in which human rights are really property rights, a sense which is much obscured in our time. Take, for example, the human right of freedom of assembly. Suppose that a certain group wants to demonstrate for a particular idea or bill in a street meeting. This is an expression of the right of assembly. On the other hand, suppose that the police break up the meeting on the ground that traffic is being disrupted. Now, it is not sufficient simply to say that the right of assembly has been abridged by the police for political reasons. Possibly, this was the case. But there is possibly a real problem, for maybe traffic was disrupted. In that case, how is one to decide between the human right of free assembly and the "public policy" or "public good" of clear and unobstructed traffic? In the face of this apparent conflict, many people conclude that rights must be relative rather than absolute and have to be curbed sometimes for the common good.

But the real problem in this matter is that the government owns the streets, which means that they are in a virtual state of nonownership. This causes not only traffic jams, but also confusion and conflict over who should use the streets at any given time. The taxpayers? In the last analysis, we are all taxpayers. Should the taxpayers who want to demonstrate be allowed to use the street for that purpose at the time they choose, or should it be reserved for use by other groups of taxpayers as motorists or pedestrians? Who is to decide? Only government can decide; and whatever it does, its decision is bound to be a wholly arbitrary one that can only aggravate and never resolve the conflict between the opposed forces. Consider, however, a situation where the streets are owned by private citizens. In this case, we see clearly that the whole question is one of property rights. If Jones owns a street and the Citizens United want to use it for a demonstration, they may offer to hire the street for that purpose. Then it is up to Jones to decide whether he will rent it out and at what price he will agree to the deal. We see that this is not really a question of the human right of the Citizens United to freedom of assembly; what is involved is their property right to use their money to offer to hire the street for the demonstration. But, in a free society, they cannot force Jones to agree; the ultimate decision is Jones', in accordance with his property right to dispose of the street as he sees fit.

Thus, we see how government ownership obscures the real issue – how it creates vague and spurious "human rights" that seemingly conflict with each other and with the "public good." In situations where all of the factors involved are owned privately, it is clear that there is no problem or conflict of human rights; on the contrary, only property rights are involved, and there is no vagueness or conflict

109

in deciding who owns what or what is permissible in any particular case.

In short, there are no human rights that are separable from property rights. The human right of free speech is only the property right to hire an assembly hall from the owner or owners by mutual agreement and to speak to those who are willing to listen and to buy materials and then print leaflets or books and sell them to those people who are willing to buy. There is no extra right of free speech beyond the property rights that we can enumerate in any given case. In all seeming cases of human rights, then, the proper course is to find and identify the property rights involved. And this procedure will resolve any apparent conflicts of rights; for property rights are always precise and legally recognizable.

Consider the classic case where "freedom of speech" is supposed to be curbed in "the public interest": Justice Holmes' famous dictum that there is no right to cry "fire" in a crowded theater. Holmes and his followers have used this illustration over and over to proclaim the supposed necessity for rights to be relative and tentative rather than absolute and eternal.

But let us further analyze this problem. The person who brings on a riot by falsely shouting "fire" in a crowded theater is, necessarily, either the owner of the theater or a paying patron. If the shouter is the owner, then he or she has committed fraud on his or her customers. The owner has taken their money in exchange for a promise to put on a movie; and now, instead, the owner disrupts the movie by falsely shouting 'fire' and breaking up the performance. The owner has thus welshed on this contractual obligation, in violation of the property rights of his or her patrons.

Suppose, on the other hand, that the shouter is a patron and not the owner. In that case, the shouter is violating the owner's property right. As a guest, he or she has access to the property on certain terms, including an obligation not to violate the owner's property right or disrupt the performance that the owner is putting on for his guests – *i.e.*, to not violate the property rights of the other guests as well. The patron's malicious act, therefore, violates the property rights of the theater owner and the property rights of all other patrons.

If we consider the problem in terms of property rights instead of the vague and woolly human right of free speech, we see that there is no conflict and no necessity of limiting or abridging rights in any way. The rights of the individual are still eternal and absolute; but they are property rights. The person who maliciously cries "fire" in a crowded theater is a criminal, not because his so-called right of free speech must be pragmatically restricted on behalf of the "public good"; he is a criminal, because he has clearly and obviously violated the property right of another person.

Notes

[1]Originally published in *Essays on Liberty* (Irvington-on-Hudson, New York: The Foundation for Economic Education, 1962), VI, p. 315.

[2]Dr. Rothbard is a Professor of Economics at the University of Nevada at Las Vegas, and is Vice-President for Academic Affairs of the Ludwig von Mises Institute,

which is also located at 322 Massachusetts Avenue, N.E., Washington, D.C. 20002, 1-202-543-7696.

Appendix VI

The Elite Under Capitalism[1]

Dr. Ludwig von Mises[2]

A long line of eminent authors, beginning with Adam Ferguson, tried to grasp the characteristic feature that distinguishes the modern capitalistic society, the market economy, from the older systems of the arrangement of social coöperation. They distinguished between warlike nations and commercial nations, between societies of a militant structure and those of individual freedom, between the society based on status and that based on contract. The appreciation of each of the two "ideal types" was, of course, different with the various authors. But they all agreed in establishing the contrast between the two types of social coöperation as well as in the cognition that no third principle of the arrangement of social affairs is thinkable and feasible.[3] One may disagree with some of the characteristics that they ascribed to each of the two types, but one must admit that the classification of such makes us comprehend essential facts of history as well as contemporary social conflicts.

There are several reasons that prevent a full understanding of the significance of the distinction between these two types of society. There is in the first place the

113

popular repugnance to assign to the inborn inequality of various individuals its due importance. There is furthermore the failure to realize the fundamental difference that exists between the meaning and the effects of private ownership of the means of production in the precapitalistic and in the capitalistic society. Finally, there is serious confusion brought about by the ambiguous employment of the term, "economic power."

The doctrine that ascribed all differences between individuals to postnatal influences is untenable. The fact that human beings are born unequal in regard to physical and mental capacities is not denied by any reasonable person, certainly also not by pediatrists. Some individuals surpass other people in health and vigor, in brain power and aptitude for various performances, in energy and resolution. Some people are better fit for the pursuit of earthly affairs, some less. From this point of view, we may – without indulging in any judgment of value – distinguish between superior and inferior people. Karl Marx referred to "unequal individual endowment and thus productive capacity as natural privileges" and was fully aware of the fact that people "would not be different individuals if they were not unequal."[4]

In the precapitalistic ages the better endowed, the "superior" people, took advantage of their superiority, by seizing power and enthralling the masses of weaker, i.e., "inferior" people. Victorious warriors appropriated to themselves all the land available for hunting and fishing, cattle raising, and tilling. Nothing was left to the rest of the people than to serve the princes and their retinue. They were serfs and slaves, landless and penniless underlings.

Such was by and large the state of affairs in most parts

of the world in the ages in which the "heroes"[5] were supreme and "commercialism" was absent. But subsequently, in a process that, although again and again frustrated by a renascence of the spirit of violence, went on for centuries and is still going on, the spirit of business – *i.e.*, of peaceful coöperation under the principle of the division of labor – undermined the mentality of the "good old days." Capitalism – the market economy – radically transformed the economic and political organization of people, in lands that adopted it to a large degree.

In the precapitalistic society, the superior people knew no other method of utilizing their own superiority than to subdue the masses of inferior people. But under capitalism the more able and more gifted people can profit from their superiority, only by serving to the best of their abilities the wishes and wants of the majority of less gifted people. In the market economy the consumers are supreme. They determine, by their buying or abstention from buying, what should be produced, by whom and how it should be produced, what quality should be produced, and what quantity should be produced. The entrepreneurs, capitalists, and landowners who fail to satisfy in the best possible and cheapest way the most urgent of the not yet satisfied wishes of the consumers are forced to go out of business and forfeit their preferred positions. In business offices and in laboratories the keenest minds are busy fructifying the most complex achievements of scientific research for the production of ever better implements and gadgets for people who have no inkling of the scientific theories that make the fabrication of such things possible. The bigger an enterprise is, the more it is forced to adjust its production activities to the changing whims and fancies of the masses,

115

its masters. The fundamental principle of capitalism is mass production to supply the masses. It is the patronage of the masses that makes enterprises grow into bigness. The common man is supreme in the market economy. He is the customer "who is always right."

In the political sphere representative government is the corollary of the supremacy of the consumers in the market. The office-holders depend on the voters in a way similar to that in which the entrepreneurs and investors depend on the consumers. The same historical process that substituted the capitalistic mode of production for precapitalistic methods substituted popular government – democracy – for royal absolutism and other forms of government by the few. And wherever the market economy is superseded by socialism, autocracy makes a comeback. It does not matter whether the socialist or communist despotism is camouflaged by the use of aliases, such as the "dictatorship of the proletariat," the "people's democracy," or the "fuhrer principle." It always amounts to a subjection of the many to the few.

It is hardly possible to misconstrue more improperly the state of affairs prevailing in the capitalistic society than by dubbing the capitalists and entrepreneurs a "ruling" class intent upon "exploiting" the masses of decent people. We do not have to raise the question of how the people who under capitalism are business operators would have tried to take advantage of their superior talents in any other thinkable organization of production activities. Under capitalism they are vying with one another in serving the masses of less gifted people. All their thoughts aim at perfecting the methods of supplying the consumers. Every year, every month, and every week, something unheard of before appears on the market and is very soon made accessible to the many. Precisely because they are producing for profit, the business operators are producing for the use of the consumers.

Confusion Concerning Property

The second deficiency of the customary treatment of the problems of society's economic organization is the confusion produced by the indiscriminate employment of juridical concepts, first of all the concept of private property.

In the precapitalistic ages there prevailed by and large economic self-sufficiency, first of every household and later – with the gradual progress toward commercialism – of small regional units. The much greater part of all products did not reach the market. They were consumed without having been sold and bought. Under such conditions there was no essential difference between private ownership of producer' goods and that of consumers' goods. In each case property served the owner exclusively. To own something, whether a producers' good or a consumers' good, meant to have it for oneself alone and to deal with it for one's own satisfaction.

But it is different in the frame of a market economy. The owner of producers' goods, the capitalist, can derive advantage from his ownership, only by employing them for the best possible satisfaction of the wants of the consumers. In the market economy, property in the means of production is acquired and preserved by serving the public and is lost, if the public becomes dissatisfied with the way in which it is served. Private property of the material factors of production is a public mandate, which is withdrawn as soon as the consumers think that other people would employ the capital goods more efficiently for their, namely the consumers', benefit. By the instrumentality of the profit and loss system, the capitalists are forced to deal with "their" property, as if it were other peoples' property entrusted to them under the obligation to utilize it for the best possible provision of the virtual beneficiaries, the consumers. This real meaning of private ownership of the material factors of production under capitalism could be ignored and misinterpreted, because all people – economists, lawyers, and lay people – had been led astray by the fact that the legal concept of property as developed by the juridical practices and doctrines of precapitalistic ages has been retained unchanged or only slightly altered while its effective meaning has been radically transformed.[6]

In the feudal society, the economic situation of every individual was determined by the share allotted to him by the powers that be. The poor man was poor because little land or no land at all had been given to him. He could with good reason think (to say it openly would have been too dangerous): I am poor because other people have more than a fair share. But, in the frame of a capitalistic society, the accumulation of additional capital, by those who succeeded in utilizing their funds for the best possible provision of the consumers, enriches not only the owners but all of the people, on the one hand by raising the marginal productivity of labor and thereby wages and on the other hand by increasing the quality of goods produced and brought to the market. The peoples of the economically backward countries are poorer than the Americans, because their countries lack a sufficient number of successful capitalists and entrepreneurs.

A tendency toward an improvement of the standard of living of the masses can prevail, only when and where the accumulation of new capital outruns the increase in population figures.

The formation of capital is a process performed with the coöperation of the consumers – *i.e.*, only those entrepreneurs can earn surpluses whose activities satisfy best the public. Once the capital is accumulated, it must be directed by anticipating the most urgent of the yet unsatisfied wishes of the consumers, to hold their coöperation in the further accumulation of capital. Thus capital comes into existence and is employed according to the wishes of the consumers.

Two Kinds of Power

When in dealing with market phenomena we apply the term, "power," we must be fully aware of the fact that we are employing it with a connotation that is entirely different from the traditional connotation attached to it in dealing with issues of government and affairs of state.

Governmental power is the faculty to beat into submission all those who would dare to disobey the orders issued by the authorities. Nobody would call government an entity that lacks this faculty. Every governmental action is backed by constables, prison guards, and executioners. However beneficial a governmental action may appear, it is ultimately made possible, only by the government's power to compel its subjects to do what many of them would not do if they were not threatened by the police and the penal courts. A government supported hospital serves charitable purposes; but the taxes collected that enable the authorities to spend money for the upkeep of the hospital are not paid voluntarily. The citizens pay taxes, because not to pay them would bring them into prison and physical resistance to the revenue agents would bring them to the gallows.

It is true that the majority of the people willy-nilly acquiesce in this state of affairs and, as David Hume put it, "resign their own sentiments and passions to those of their rulers."[7] They proceed in this way, because they think that in the long run they serve better their own interests by being loyal to their government than by overturning it. But this does not alter the fact that governmental power means the exclusive faculty to frustrate any disobedience by the recourse to violence. As human nature is, the institution of government is an indispensable means to make civilized life possible. The alternative is anarchy and the law of the stronger. But the fact remains that government is the power to imprison and to kill.

The concept of economic power as applied by the socialist authors means something entirely different. The fact to which it refers is the capacity to influence the behavior of other people by offering them something, the acquisition of which they consider as more desirable than the avoidance of the sacrifice they have to make for it. In plain words: It means the invitation to enter into a bargain, an act of exchange. I will give you *a* if you give me *b*. There is no question of any compulsion nor of any threats. The buyer does not "rule" the seller and the seller does not "rule" the buyer.

Of course, in the market economy everyone's style

of life is adjusted to the division of labor, and a return to self sufficiency is out of the question. Everyone's bare survival would be jeopardized, if suddenly everyone were forced to experience the autarky of ages gone by; but, in the regular course of market transactions, there is no danger of such a relapse into the conditions of the primeval household economy. A faint image of the effects of any disturbance in the usual course of market exchanges is provided when labor union violence, benevolently tolerated or even openly encouraged and aided by the government, stops the activities of vital branches of government.

In the market economy every specialist – and there are no other people than specialists – depends on all other specialists. This mutuality is the characteristic feature of interpersonal relations under capitalism. The socialists ignore the fact of mutuality and speak of economic power. For example, as they see it, "the capacity to determine product" is one of the powers of the entrepreneur.[8] One can hardly misconstrue more radically the essential features of the market economy. It is not business, but the consumers who ultimately determine what should be produced. It is a silly fable that nations go to war because there is a munitions industry and that people are getting drunk because the distillers have "economic power." If one calls economic power the capacity to choose – or, as the socialists prefer to say, the power to "determine" – the product, one must establish the fact that this power is fully vested in the buyers and consumers.

"Modern civilization, nearly all civilization," said the great British economist, Edwin Cannan, "is based on the principle of making things pleasant for those who please the market and unpleasant for those who fail to do so."[9]

The market means the buyers; the consumers means all of the people. To the contrary, under planning or socialism the goals of production are determined by the supreme planning authority; the individual gets what the authority thinks the individual ought to get. All of this empty talk about the economic power of business aims at obliterating this fundamental distinction between freedom and bondage.

The "Power" of the Employer

People also refer to economic power in describing the internal conditions prevailing within the various enterprises. The owner of a private firm or the president of a corporation, it is said, enjoys within his outfit absolute power. He is free to indulge in his whims and fancies. All employees depend on his arbitrariness. They must stoop and obey or else face dismissal and starvation.

Such observations, too, ascribe to the employers powers that are vested in the consumers. The requirement to outstrip its competitors by serving the public in the cheapest and best possible way enjoins upon every enterprise the necessity to employ the personnel best fitted for the performance of the various functions entrusted to them. The individual enterprise must try to outdo its competitors, not only by the employment of the most suitable methods of production and the purchase of the best fitted materials but also by hiring the right type of workers. It is true that the head of an enterprise has the faculty to give vent to his sympathies or antipathies. He is free to prefer an inferior man to a better man; he may fire a valuable assist-

122

ant and in his place employ an incompetent and inefficient substitute. But all the faults he commits in this regard affect the profitability of his enterprise. He has to pay for them in full. It is the very supremacy of the market that penalizes such capricious behavior. The market forces the entrepreneurs to deal with every employee exclusively from the point of view of the services that he or she renders to the satisfaction of the consumers.

What curbs in all market transactions the temptation of indulging in malice and venom is precisely the costs involved in such behavior. The consumer is free to boycott for some reasons, popularly called noneconomic or irrational, the purveyor who would in the best and cheapest way satisfy his wants. But then he has to bear the consequences; he will either be less perfectly served or he will have to pay a higher price. Civil government enforces its commandments, by recourse to violence or the threat of violence. The market does not need any recourse to violence, because neglect of its rationality penalizes itself.

The critics of capitalism fully acknowledge this fact, in pointing out that for private enterprise nothing counts but the striving after profit. Profit can be made only by satisfying the consumers better or cheaper or better and cheaper than others do. The consumer has in his capacity as customer the right to be full of whim and fancies. The business operator as producer has only one aim: to provide for the consumer. If one deplores the business person's unfeeling preoccupation with profit-seeking, one has to realize two things. First, that this attitude is prescribed to the entrepreneur by the consumers who are not prepared to accept any excuse for poor service. Secondly, that it is precisely this neglect of "the human angle" that prevents arbitrariness and partiality from affecting the employer-employee nexus.

A Duty of the Elite

To establish these facts does not amount either to a commendation or to a condemnation of the market economy or its political corollary, government by the people (representative government or democracy). Science is neutral with regard to any judgments of value. It neither approves nor condemns; it just describes and analyzes what is.

Stressing the fact that under unhampered capitalism the consumers are supreme in determining the goals of production does not imply any opinion about the moral and intellectual capacities of these individuals. The individuals, both as consumers and as voters, are mortal people who are liable to error and who may very often choose what in the long run will harm them. Philosophers may be right in severely criticizing the conduct of their fellow citizens. But there is, in a free society, no other means to avoid the evils resulting from the bad judgment of people than to induce them to alter their ways of life voluntarily. Where there is freedom, this is the task incumbent upon the elite.

People are unequal and the inherent inferiority of the many manifests itself also in the manner in which they enjoy the affluence that capitalism bestows upon them. It would be a boon for humanity, say many authors, if the common person would spend less time and money for the satisfaction of vulgar appetites and more time and money for higher and nobler gratifications. But should not the distinguished critics blame themselves rather than blame the masses? Why did they, to whom fate and nature have blessed with moral and intellectual eminence, not better succeed in persuading the masses of inferior people to drop their vulgar tastes and habits? If something is wrong with the behavior of the many, the fault rest no more with the inferiority of the masses than with the inability or unwillingness of the elite to induce all other people to accept their own higher standards of value. The serious crisis of our civilization is caused not only by the shortcomings of the masses. It is no less the effect of a failure of the elite.

Notes

[1]This essay was originally published in *The Freeman*, XII (January, 1962), 3.

[2]At the time of this writing, Dr. Mises was Visiting Professor of Economics at New York University and part-time adviser, consultant, and staff member of the Foundation for Economic Education.

Dr. Mises is the most capable economist in human history and has been ignored and suppressed but not refuted. If his great message in his many works is not carefully studied, correctly interpreted, and diligently applied, we will lose this civilization. JEN.

[3]Ludwig von Mises, *Human Action: A Treatise on Economics* (New Haven: Yale University Press, 1949), pp. 196-199.

[4]Karl Marx and Frederick Engels, *Selected Works* (Moscow: Progress Publishers, 1970), III, 18.

[5]Werner Sombart, *Handler und Helden: Patriotifche Befinnungen* (Munich and Leipzip: Dunker & Humbolt, 1915). The title in English is *Traders and Heroes: Patriotic Consciousness.*

[6]It was the great Roman poet, Quintus Horatius Flaccus, who first alluded to this characteristic feature of property of producers' goods in a market economy. Ludwig von Mises, *Socialism: An Economic and Sociological Analysis*, trans. J. Kahne (Indianapolis: Liberty Fund, 1981), p. 31 n.

[7]David Hume, *Essays: Moral, Political, and Literary* (Indianapolis: Liberty Fund, 1985), p. 32.

[8]Adolph A. Berle, Jr., *Power without Property* (New York: Harcourt, Brace, Inc., 1959), p. 82.

[9]Edwin Cannan, *An Economist's Protest* (New York: Adelphi Co., 1928), pp. vi-vii.

Appendix VII

Let George Do It?

James Ervin Norwood

With such strangers to the Constitution as *Missouri v. Holland*, supra, *U.S. v. Belmont*, supra, *U.S. v. Pink*, supra, and *U.S. v. Curtiss-Wright*, supra, as precedents, only public opinion (which is not beyond manipulation), and practical considerations stand between the Executive branch and rule by decree, which means dictatorship. By executive agreements with foreign powers, the Executive branch could nationalize every nut and bolt in the U.S. economy and could seize and redistribute land holdings, not to mention all other property and indeed the people themselves.[1]

You might say that such deals would be made with the advice and consent of two-thirds of the Politburo by a Pinko in the White House and that they would be enforced on an economically depressed, disorganized, demoralized, drugged, and militarily surrounded American people by the communist armies externally and by a Red Guerrilla Army, a communist-infiltrated judiciary, and a communist-controlled bureaucracy and police internally.

These surrenders on the installment plan would be aided, abetted, and egged on by Red infiltration of and influence in the media, the publishing houses (including especially textbook publishing outfits in the social sciences), police, schools and universities, seminaries, churches and synagogues, lodges and clubs, and professional associations.

Many secret executive agreements with foreign powers, including the U.S.S.R., now have the force of law – secret, deadly, unconstitutional law. A former head of the State Department Treaty Staff, Bryton Barron, wrote on this as follows:

> As the head of the treaty staff I learned of the existence of a very large number of secret agreements which our government had worked out with other nations, concerning the nature of which you and even members of the United States Senate had little idea. I was never too sure that even the responsible officials in the Department were always informed as to all of the treaties and executive agreements that apply to their respective areas of concern. I recall, for example, a meeting that was held in my office in the late 40's, attended by ranking officials from the various political areas, at which it was pointed out that there were a number of secret agreements in force with other countries concerning which these officials were apparently unaware. Such a situation is highly disturbing.[2]

Among these secret executive agreements with foreign powers having the force of law as treaties are the ultra-secret, multi-national Nogod Case Agreements made by Franklin D. Roosevelt and Harry S. Truman, under which more than one American citizen's property was seized and

128

under which the liberty of many Americans has been compromised.[3]

Secret executive agreements, such as the patently illegal and horrible Nogod Case Agreements, that violate the Constitution, under the cover of the mistaken doctrine that the provisions of treaties and executive agreements in conflict with the Constitution and subsequent enabling legislation in conflict with the Constitution are supreme to the Constitution, would have been impossible had the Treaty Clause been correctly read and had the Constitution been adhered to, which must occur to nullify such agreements and to prevent the recurrence of such agreements.[4]

Notes

[1]As to the redistribution of land holdings, such a movement is already in the mill. One can pick up the drift of the matter from the following references: *Midkiff v. Tom*, 471 F. Supp. 871 (1979); *Midkiff v. Tom*, 483 F. Supp. 62 (1979); *Midkiff v. Tom*, 702 F. 2nd 788 (1983); *Hawaii Housing Authority v. Midkiff*, 463 U.S. 1323, 77 L. Ed. 2nd 1426, 104 S. Ct. 7 (1983); *Midkiff v. Tom*, 464 U.S. 932, 78 L. Ed. 2nd 304, 104 S. Ct. 334 (1983); *Midkiff v. Tom*, 725 F. 2nd 502 (1984); and *Hawaii Housing Authority v. Midkiff*, 467 U.S. 229, 81 L. Ed. 2nd 186, 104 S. Ct. 2321 (1984).

[2]Bryton Barron, *Inside the State Department* (New York: Communication Services, 1956), pp. 116-117.

[3]One tangible handle to the Nogod Case Agreements is the CIA's MK-ULTRA operation, in which

some of the victims were tortured and drugged to sense-lessness. *i.e.*. They were driven out of their minds, so as to destroy their credibility as witnesses and to destroy their competence generally.

Dr. Mary Matilda Morrow, M.D., a Canadian psychiatrist who practices psychiatry in Ogdenburg, New York, is one of the victims of MK-ULTRA, about which the CIA burned its records to frustrate investigations and law suits, and is an incidental victim of the Nogod Case. Today, she is miserable, having been brutally "treated" with electric shock to her brain and with LSD in Dr. Sidney Gottlieb's torture chamber in Montreal, Ontario, Canada.

Dr. Gottlieb, M.D., a Canadian psychiatrist, was a principal contractor for the CIA in the MK-ULTRA Operation and in the Nogod Case and worked on the Nogod Case as early as the fall of 1948 in Texas.

Dr. P. G. Nogod, M.D., an American psychiatrist, and his wife, Mary Catherine, also an American psychiatrist, were making noise about the government's criminal operations in medicine and other fields and had to be silenced with the infamous Nogod Case Agreements, which "legalized" their torture and brainwashing on American soil and the obliteration of their personal and professional records.

It is to the external disgrace of the United States Supreme Court that all nine "Justices" played ball with the United States Government on the Nogod Case Agreements. When the chips were down, the fine nine bedded down with the rattlesnakes and became criminals themselves. (The idea that we have an independent judiciary is largely a myth. The Supreme Court has turned the Constitution into a scrap of paper for the government

130

and the Congress.)

Is it any wonder that Bryton Barron was harassed out of the State Department for getting inquisitive about secret treaties? Was he getting close to the suppressed Nogod Film Series of chronological motion pictures that give an extremely interesting, entertaining, and informative historical perspective to the Nogod Case Agreements? How close did he get to the top-level criminal conspirators in and out of the three branches of government who supported the Nogod Case Agreements to nullify the Constitutional rights of many Americans under the cloak of "national security"?

[4]The exposure of the Nogod Case Agreements would do much to generate a popular demand for the limitation of government power to constitutional proscriptions, as everyone is either a direct or indirect victim of the agreements.

The photograph that follows this note is relevant to breaking the U.S. Government's cover-up on the Nogod Case Agreements. The photograph contradicts much of the government's gigantic lie in relation to the agreements and thus leads to wiping out the rest of its fib.

The photograph places the author in World War II, which fact the government has tried to cover up. When the government got word that a search of military records was being planned to get copies of special orders that were issued in World War II with the author's name on them, its agents burned down the military records center at St. Louis, Missouri. The government carefully purged the author's name from official military unit histories, took pains to keep his name out of unofficial unit histories and other accounts of the war, and destroyed combat film footage that the author occasionally appeared in. The government

131

destroyed the academic and professional records of the author and licenses that would accurately identify the author.

To remove the author from public attention, the government subjected him to a forced change of legal and psychological identity. To make its criminal operation stick, the government subjected the author to a brutal brainwashing and induced amnesia with hypnosis (the disastrous result of which was a dual personality); and the government fabricated records and attributed them to the author.

With comments to the media by comrades of the author on the battlefields of World War II and Korea and in military activities between those wars, the government's Nogod Case Agreements will be broken open for public scrutiny and general condemnation; and they will collapse on top of the criminal conspirators that put them together and bury them deep in the dungeons of the blackest pages of American history.

Major General John H. Hester (left, C.G. of the 43rd Division), Colonel James Ervin "Piggi" Norwood (on General Hester's left), Major Phillip E. Rose (Division Signal Officer, on Colonel Norwood's left), and First Lieutenant George E. Skelton (right, Signal Construction Officer), discuss location for the Command Post and Message Center on New Georgia, July 6, 1943.

Colonel Norwood – a precocious, multi-skilled and multi-mission, get-it-done trouble shooter – also served with other units of the Army and with various units of the Army Air Force, the Marine Corps, and the Navy during the war.

Colonel Norwood held higher grades at times.

Appendix VIII

The Marxian Conquest of the World and Our Strategy for Victory

James Ervin Norwood

How are we being taken by the communists? What is happening, why is it happening, and what can we do about it before we reach any one of several points of no return? Had Khruschev said, "You are burying yourselves," he would have been right.

Conventional War Is Unlikely

The communists dare not attack all-out with conventional forces, for they do not have the mass of dedicated people – people who will die and suffer in large numbers to defend and advance communism – to conduct a large-scale conventional war. In World War II, an entire division defected to the Germans and fought to defeat the communists. (The dependents of the defectors joined the troops in their flight from communist tyranny.) Crowds of people in the cities initially turned out to greet German troops with cheers and flowers, welcoming them as liberators. The people were soon whipped into a frenzy of opposition to the Germans by German atrocities, some of which were faked by communists in German uniforms, filmed, shown to the Russian people, and blamed on the Germans to stir up the Russian people.

The communists do not have the resources for a sustained conventional war. Their meager socialist economies would rapidly crumble without Western aid and loans and without imports. Their bureaucratic mismanagement of their economies is the equivalent of our strategic bombardment of them with conventional ordnance, which would not even be necessary for their collapse.[1]

Nuclear War Is Unlikely

The communists are smart enough not to punch through our atomic Maginot line for a quick kill. They know that to do so would result in their destruction as well as our desctruction. Although one side or the other might win militarily, it would lose in every other respect. (I suspect that the end result would be a war of attrition with bows and arrows.) They want to take us in one piece, in working order. They do not want to destroy what they figure they will some day own.

Purposes of Communist Military Power

The communists maintain enormous conventional and nuclear forces for several reasons. Their conventional arm serves to keep their captive populations in line, to sup-

136

port paramilitary operations, and to suppress rebellion and revoltuion in the communist camp. Their nuclear forces are primarily used to cover paramilitary operations with the threat of a holocaust if they are opposed realistically (which threat is a total bluff), and to put false teeth in their diplomacy with their nuclear bluff. Both conventional and nuclear forces are designed to create a facade or illusion of great national power and strength that does not exist and cannot exist in a nation with a socialist economy that is unsupported by relatively free economies.

The Communist Juggernaut

Their main avenue of attack is through the human mind. Both initiation of and success in paramilitary operations depend on success in the mind war. The defense of the territories that they hold depends on success in the mind war – *i.e.*, with defeat in the mind war, the entire communist offensive threat and defensive stance will collapse overnight. Upon our victory in the brain krieg, there will be a revision of Western timidity, indecision, vacillation, slack-jawed diplomacy, flaccidity, and downright featherbedding in dealing with the communists. Western aid and government-guaranteed loans will come to a screeching halt, as muddle-headed Marxian politicians in the West are booted out of office by more intelligent electorates; and the communist economies and strategic and tactical nuclear and conventional forces will crumble, for lack of material support. (It will take all they have to half-feed their people.) Paramilitary operations will cease, as communism dies on the vine without intellectual roots to

137

support its rotten fruit. The communist leaders that survive the intellectual assault against the false premises of communism will be hard-pressed to stay in power and off the ends of ropes hanging from lamp lanyards, as billions of starving people will move to wipe them out and organize alternative forms of government that allow them the freedom to produce and eat.

Victory

Victory in the mind war must be ours, if we are to survive and defeat the communist psychosis that threatens to destroy our civilization.[2] Victory is well within our grasp. We need only attack them immediately intellectually and think to win. We must use our intellects and induce them to use their intellects to discover and buy capitalism. Whoever wins the intellectuals will win this war. (If the communists win it, they will "win" the end of civilization.)

We are in the middle of World War III. It is being fought with ideas. The battlefield stretches from your left ear to your right ear.

The professors in the social science courses in the universities control the strategic choke points. They rule the world, by instilling the premises for public policies in the minds of the future mechanics of history – the future generals and admirals, the future politicians and statesmen, the future lawyers and judges, the future business leaders, and the future government administrators. They also instill the premises for public policies in the minds of the future thought leaders – the future preachers, teachers and replacement professors in the social sciences, economists, editors, economic journalists, news columnists and commentators, newswriters, newscasters, historians, novelists, playwrights, scriptwriters, and philosophers. These professors ultimately control the production of ideas that serve as premises for public policies and thus they determine the course of history.

As the communists have assured by calculated design and action, these professors in the social sciences think from Marxian premises. This is the result of the fact that ideas from the works of Marx and his disciples have been thoroughly infiltrated for generations into the social science textbooks and thus into the teaching of the social sciences.[3]

The Marxian premises that these professors instill in their gullible victims will be championed by the future thought leaders and will be projected into public policies by the future mechanics of history, just as they are presently championed by the thought leaders and projected into public policies by the mechanics of history that went through the Marxian whirlpools in the universities. Thus have we been burying ourselves under Marxian garbage for some several generations. This process will continue to the end of our civilization in the relatively near future, unless we purposefully and aggressively take charge and reverse it.

By reaching the university professors in the social sciences and the intellectuals and thought leaders in general with the ideology of free capitalistic enterprise and equality before the law, we can defeat communism, save ourselves and civilization, and promote prosperity and universal peace. One good way to do this is to offer book scholarships to students and student intellectuals, to professors and teachers in the social sciences, and to thought leaders.

Our road to victory is paved with the works of Dr. Ludwig von Mises. (The works of his disciples, many of which are in the bibliography in Appendix II, also deserve our attention.) Mises refutes Marxian social theories and offers us a positive alternative in the ideology of free capitalistic enterprise and equality before the law. By studying Mises (and his disciples) carefully and projecting his social theories into public policies, we will see peace and a better and more prosperous world by the turn of this century. Mises is more than a match for Marx.

Victory requires human action with and from *Human Action*,[4] *Socialism*,[5] *Theory of Money and Credit*,[6] and the other great works of the incomparable Mises,[7] the greatest thinker in economics in human history. If you will bring the big guns of Ludwig Edler von Mises into action,[8] I will guarantee you Victory.[9]

Notes

[1]The purpose of strategic bombing is to cause accelerated capital attrition. We can achieve the same result in communist-ruled countries, by simply cutting off foreign aid to them and by knocking off government-guaranteed loans to them. As they consume their capital in pursuit of their socialist delusions, their economies will fall apart. So far, they have survived largely by Western aid and loans.

[2]One can find a diagnosis and a prognosis of the communists in the work of the Australian psychiatrist, Dr. Fred Schwarz, *You Can Trust the Communists – To Be*

Communists (Englewood Cliffs, New Jersey: Prentice-Hall, Inc., 1960). Although most of the economics in this work is flawed, the diagnosis and the prognosis are right on target. Therefore, this work should be carefully read and used to the utmost in winning the mind war. Dr. Schwarz is the world's leading authority on the psychotic nature of communist thinking.

Dr. Schwarz is the Director of the Christian Anti-Communism Crusade, P.O. Box 890, Long Beach, California 90801, 1-213-437-0941. He publishes up-to-date reports on the communist threat in his newsletter.

[3]I was visiting with Dr. Howard Kershner, noted author and foreign missionary, at Northwood Institute, Cedar Hill, Texas, in January of 1980. He told me about a conference he had had in the Kremlin with a high communist official. It went as follows:

Soviet Minister: Ha! Ha! Ha! We are going to defeat you!

Dr. Kershner: What makes you so sure?

Soviet Minister: Do you see these books on the shelf behind me?

Dr. Kershner: Yes.

Soviet Minister: They are used to teach the students in your universities. *We wrote them.*

I had already worked out the logic of the Kremlin's approach, by comparing the writings of Marx and Lenin with the contents of the textbooks in the social sciences and by observing their expression in the media and their projection in public policies. Dr. Kershner's conference with the Soviet Minister dramatized the logic authoritatively.

[4]Ludwig von Mises, *Human Action: A Treatise on Economics* (Chicago: Henry Regnery Co., 1966).

[5]Ludwig von Mises, *Socialism: an Economic and Sociological Analysis*, trans. J. Kahane (Indianapolis: Liberty Fund, 1981).

[6]Ludwig von Mises, *Theory of Money and Credit*, trans. H. E. Batson (Irvington-on-Hudson, New York: The Foundation for Economic Education, 1971).

[7]Bibliography, Appendix II.

[8]Action means reading his works, to the extent that you have the time, intelligence, temperament, and interest to do so. It also means, if you are a teacher in the social sciences, asking your students to read books by Mises for extra credit. Action includes giving books to students, teachers, and others who say that they will read them and who will accept them as gifts. Action means financing one-year sabbaticals for thought leaders to read Mises and making tax-deductible grants through foundations to intellectuals for their extended study of Mises. Action means placing the works of Mises in libraries, both public and academic. Action includes endowing chairs in universities and colleges for Misesian scholars to reach students with the Great Misesian Message of Meritocracy with Free Capitalistic Enterprise and Equality before the Law.

[9]The Misesian Revolution will sweep the world, will wipe out war, and will enable us to raise ourselves and our civilization to unimaginable heights in a global free market.

Appendix IX

The High Frontier

James Ervin Norwood

The argument over Star Wars will keep blowing and going, until the Russians get their star wars operational. Then we can only want to get our Star Wars operational, for the Russians will put their thermonuclear gun to our heads to stop us from doing so.

The Russians have a high priority, super-secret crash program in the mill to beat us to the punch on Star Wars, so that they can use it to put unbreakable nuclear teeth in their diplomatic demands and a credible nuclear cover over their paramilitary and conventional military operations. Meanwhile, they are conducting a massive propaganda campaign in our media to convince us that Star Wars won't work, so that we won't get it up before they do.

If we want to live in the next century under the Stars and Stripes instead of suffer and die under the Hammer and Sickle, we would be well advised to get Star Wars tested and operational not later than yesterday.[1] If we let the Russians win this race, the ball game is over, both militarily and diplomatically. They will simply extort surrender on the installment plan in a series of concessions.

General Daniel O. Graham, U.S.A. Retired, former

Director of the Defense Intelligence Agency, supports Star Wars;[2] Major General George Keegan, USAF, Retired, former Director of Air Force Intelligence, supports Star Wars; and our Joint Chiefs of Staff support Star Wars. Who else supports Star Wars? The Politburo.

It follows that our civil defense structure must be adequate to pull any remaining nuclear teeth from Soviet diplomacy; *i.e.*, our civil defense must be adequate to protect us from any missiles that might get through High Frontier and a back-up ABM[3] filter system.

You can believe that the dentists in the Kremlin have both an ABM system and a civil defense operation to complement and make fully effective their Star Wars scheme to turn us into a toothless tiger at the conference table.

Aside from Star Wars, an ABM system, and a realistic civil defense, what is missing from our diplomacy are tenacious and wise leaders dedicated to the destruction of communism and the construction of capitalism. We can get those determined and intelligent leaders with book wars. This is not a top-to-bottom operation that begins with others; it is a bottom-to-top operation that begins with you. So, when you get right down to it, what is missing from our diplomacy is your active contribution to it – *i.e.*, your condemnation of flip-flop expediency and accomodations to Marxism and your demand that we key our diplomacy unswervingly to the goal of Victory.[4]

Notes

[1]Daniel O. Graham, *We Must Defend America and Put an End to MADness* (Chicago: Regnery Gateway; and

Falls Church, Virginia: Conservative Press, 1983).

MAD is the acronym for mutually assured destruction. One could call such an incredible policy HAD with MAD – home assured destruction with mutually assured destruction.

[2]If you wish to work with General Graham in supporting Star Wars, you can get further information on films, publications, tapes, and the like from his base of operations, which is as follows: High Frontier, 1010 Vermont Avenue, Suite 1000, Washington, D.C. 20005, 1-202-737-4979.

General Graham, with your help, can get Star Wars up to block diplomatic shakedowns, maintain military peace, and make Victory possible on the ideological front.

[3]Anti-ballistic missile.

[4]The first three paragraphs of this essay appeared in the *Waco Tribune-Herald*, July 28, 1987, p. 4A. The author's letter containing the three paragraphs was written on July 7, 1987. The letter was immediately used to develop this appendix.

Appendix X

Pearl Harbor II[1]

James Ervin Norwood

Only someone who has never studied and understood the writings of Vladimir Lenin would go for any kind of a disarmament deal with the Soviets.

The Soviets always tie such arrangements to their diplomacy and never have the slightest intention of keeping them intact any longer than they are useful for that purpose and thus for the objective of communist conquest of the world. For them to behave otherwise would be an illogical betrayal of their definition of what is moral.[2]

We tie such pacts to domestic politics and honor them as a matter of law.

One result of the disaster of December 8, 1987, will be to turn Western Eurpoe into a gigantic Finland that is open to swift conquest and thus to diplomatic intimidation and military neutralization. Another result of Pearl Harbor II will be to brand the United States once again, as an undependable and unpredictable ally that charts its course by the winds of public opinion that the communists can and do easily manipulate with the help of their witting and unwitting allies in the media.

The Pershing II missile is easy to move and hide and

147

is thus hard to find and hit, in contrast to fixed-position missiles. The Pershing can hit Soviet command centers and fixed-position missiles, not to mention industrial targets, within eight minutes from launch.

To throw away the Pershing Peacekeeper for a Leninist pie-crust treaty that is made to be broken borders on psychosis.[3]

Although the issues between East and West must ultimately be settled on an ideological plane if all are to win, it is my opinion that we must remain strong enough to make the world safe for debate.

Notes

[1]Nearly all of this essay was in the author's letter to the *Waco Tribune-Herald*, December 22, 1987, p. 4 A.

[2]Schwarz, *op. cit.*

[3]"You know that treaties and laws are worth nothing but a scrap of paper in the face of international conflicts." V. I. Lenin, *Collected Works* (Moscow: Progress Publishers, 1965), XXVII, 368.

Appendix XI

Modern War

James Ervin Norwood

Speaking from the point of view of one who has been on his share of battlefields, I find the present World Ideological War much more difficult to deal with than all previous wars that I have fought in combined. In this conflict, victory cannot be achieved with the simple application of force of arms. A true trumph can come only from an industrious and sustained application of mind power. Mind power is to World War III as the combination of air, sea, and ground power was to World War II – decisive.[1]

All physical wars are, in my opinion, projections of unresolved ideological conflicts. If one side or if both sides resolve them into a consensus of values, a physical war is, by the above definition, impossible. Why fight, if there is nothing to fight about?

With the loss of civilization as the alternative to the defeat of collectivism, it is important that intellectuals on both sides win this war – i.e., resolve this conflict of ideologies – for property rights and the free market.[2] Peace – real peace – can come only with that Victory.[3] With that awesome task accomplished, we can stack arms

149

and truly say *farewell to arms*.

Notes

[1]The basic ingredients for winning remain the same – a belief in one's cause, a willingness to fight for it against an antithetical cause, and a leadership that is determined to win. That orientation is what the communists now have; and it is what we must develop as rapidly as possible. The side that has it will win; the side that lacks it will lose. As we acquire that orientation with diligent study, we must deprive the communists of it, by intellectually undermining and refuting their fallacious ideology and inducing them to believe our ideology.

[2]The Truth is on our side, if we simply learn it, sell it, and apply it.

[3]The so-called "glasnost" is the same old Leninist booze with a different label. After painful and expensive hangovers from "Peaceful Coexistence I" and the "New Economic Policy" of Lenin's day, "Peaceful Coexistence II" in the midst of Khruschev's noise, and an illogical and delusional détente in the face of the Vietnam War, we are again reaching nervously for the bottle.

When will we ever learn that there will be no peace with the communists until we defeat communism? All of the disarmament dreams, peace conferences, and the like are nothing but *evasions* of responsibility from facing the job that we must sooner or later accomplish, the destruction of communism, or be destroyed by communism.

While the communists have a plan to win and are executing that plan, we are giving them all of the help that

150

we can with government-guaranteed loans, foreign aid, and outright surrenders. Although they have published their strategy and tactics, our leaders have not bothered to read about them in the writings of the communist theoreticians. They would prefer to fly blind and interpret tactics as strategy or interpret economically and diplomatically necessitated retreats as abandonment of their psychotic goals of world conquest, the perfection of the environment, and the creation of a perfect communist man in a perfect communist world. (Schwarz, *op. cit.*)

What has been pouring forth from the State Department and the White House is not foreign policy that is based on reality. It is fantasy that borders on criminal negligence; and it indicates not merely leftist influence and control of our Ship of State through academia and the media but also an infiltration of Marxists-Leninists – *i.e.*, our pall bearers – into our policy-making bodies.

Appendix XII

The Soldier[1]

J. G. Adams

A Soldier! a soldier! I'm longing to be:
The name and the life of a soldier for me!
I would not be living at ease and at play;
True honor and glory I'd win in my day.

A soldier! a soldier! in armor arrayed;
My weapons in hand, of no contest afraid;
I'd ever be ready to strike the first blow,
And to fight my way through the ranks of the foe.

But then, let me tell you, no blood would I shed,
No victory seek o'er the dying and dead;
A far braver soldier than this would I be;
A warrior for Truth, in the ranks of the free.

A soldier! a soldier! Oh, then, let me be!
My friends, I invite you, enlist now with me.
Truth's bands shall be mustered, love's foes shall
    give way!
Let's up, and be clad in our battle array!

153

Note

[1]J. G. Adams, "The Soldier," *McGuffey's Third Eclectic Reader* (rev. ed.; New York, Cincinnati, and Chicago: American Book Co., 1896), p. 82.

Appendix XIII

The New Guard

James Ervin Norwood

Today's Warrior must persistently study the great writings in constitutional law, classical liberal political science, free market economics, history, philosophy, logic, religion, literature, and human relations. He must make progressive studies of mathematics and the physical sciences, to facilitate interpretation of writings that are in terms of those sciences to some degree and to enable him or her to make applications of those sciences in a chosen profession or skill. He must be an interpreter and a dispenser of ideologies, for Victory is not to be found in the crude use of force of arms but in the skillful use of good ideas to replace bad ideas. In essence, he must be a super salesman, a patient persuader with a better alternative to sell to those who believe what he is trying to replace. He must be literate in the principal languages of the social and physical sciences – German, French, and English – and be able to interpret Greek and Latin. He must be a logical thinker. He must be a versatile writer and speaker. He must be a scholar and a teacher, who is armed with books and ideas instead of bombs. In making war, he or she must wage peace, must deal with the formation of public opin-

155

ion in support of proven propositions that constitute sound premises for public policies – *i.e.*, public policies that make peace possible if not inevitable. His strategic aims are to eliminate the ideological causes of war as we have known it; to replace those faulty ideologies with the ideological prerequisites for peace; and thus to eliminate war and produce peace, by identifying, condemning, and eliminating popular, widely accepted, highly commended, sometimes more subtle, and often more destructive forms of aggression than war is and that lead to war. His tactical aims are to induce people to recognize these forms of aggression, which are often disguised as being for the public "good"; to recognize that those Trojan Horses of War are harmful to their self interests and prosperity; and to repudiate those deadly aggressions and any politician who supports them. His most important target, a target that he can always hit, is himself. By constantly saturating himself with better ideas, he stands ready to offer a better way to those who wish to learn with him and to campaign with him. He aggressively pursues his goal of peace but does not try to force his beliefs on anyone, knowing that that is impossible and would be immoral were it possible. He or she seeks both converts and colleagues, realizing that few in the division of labor have the time, interest, intelligence, and talent to fight it through to Victory and respecting others in the division of labor who are doing their parts to keep things going. He or she is a member of the New Guard, an elite corps of intellectual Warriors.

The mission of the New Guardian is to study, understand, develop, and promulgate in popular phraseology, as well as in abstract terms, valid premises for public policies, with the end purposes of achieving domestic tran-

156

quility and international peace.

The field marshals in the New Guard must be participants in activities requiring coöperation with others and in activities requiring coöperation from others in their student years and thereafter, as they must be followers who can coöperate with others and leaders who can get the coöperation of others.

Private funds and private funds alone must support the New Guard, as it must be free and independent of government control.

The New Guard must control the government, by influencing public opinion for a free market and minimum government. *The Power is in the People.*

Appendix XIV

Notepad

Indices

Cases

Books, Periodicals,
Essays, Reports, and Articles

Persons

190

Subjects

193

the Resumption of Friendly Relations, 75
Foundation for Economic Education, 99
Friends of Freedom Publishers, ii

General Agreement between the Government of the
    United States of America and the Government of the
    Union of Soviet Socialist Republics on Contacts, Ex-
    changes and Coöperation in Scientific, Technical,
    Educational, Cultural and other Fields, The, 86-87
General Welfare Clause, ix, 30, 37-40, 42-53, 85
Governmental power, 119-120

High Frontier, 145
Human rights and property rights, relationship between,
    103-111

Ideological war, 83-87, 89-102, 105-106, 149-153,
    155-157
Inequality of people, inherent, 104
Inherent
    external sovereignty, doctrine of, 21-23, 63-75, 78-79
    inequality of people, 104
Institute for Humane Studies, 102

Juridical concept of private property, 117-119

Laissez Faire Books, 99
Liberty Tree Network, 99
Litvinov Assignment, 5-10, 15-17
Ludwig von Mises Institute, 99, 111

Marbury v. Madison, ix, 11, 24-27, 30-31